WALKS
on the
Northumberland Coast

A guide to nine walks
of between three and seven miles in length
on and near the Northumberland coast
and one linear coastal walk of twenty five miles.

C000192306

Produced and published by
Northumberland County Council
National Park and Countryside Department
Eastburn, South Park, Hexham, Northumberland.

Text & photography by Tony Hopkins
Designed and illustrated by Brian Waters
Maps by Peter Howe

The author would like to thank the many people who offered advice or
information in the preparation of this book, in particular Peter Davies
and Don Leslie who offered many useful facts and anecdotes; also to
Dr. D.A. Robson, Dr. P. Morrison, Tony Tynan, Ted Nixon, Northumberland
County Records Office, the National Trust and Nature Conservancy Council.

Aerial Photograph of Dunstanburgh Castle pp 4/5 Department of Photography
University of Newcastle upon Tyne.

ISBN 0 907632 07 6

Typesetting by ARTYPE, 13 North Terrace, Claremont Road, Newcastle upon Tyne NE2 4BA.
Printed by HINDSON PRINT, Strawberry Place, Newcastle upon Tyne NE99 1PO.

Contents

Introduction   1
Rights of way and using this booklet   2
About the Northumberland Coast   4
The Coastal Walks   5
Walk 1 Alnmouth-Lesbury   6-10
Walk 2 Craster-Howick   11-16
Walk 3 Dunstan Steads-Craster   17-21
Walk 4 Bamburgh-Budle Point   22-25
Walk 5 Budle-Budle Point   26-29
Walk 6 Holy Island:
Lindisfarne Priory-Emanuel Head   30-34
The Inland Walks   35
Walk 7 Holburn Grange-Swinhoe Farm   36-40
Walk 8 Old Bewick-Blawearie   41-45
Walk 9 Bewick Moor: Quarryhouse to Harehope   46-51
The Northumberland Coast Walk;
Alnmouth-Budle   52-81
Glossary   82
For Further Reading   83

WITH TWENTY ONE 1:25000 (2½'') MAPS

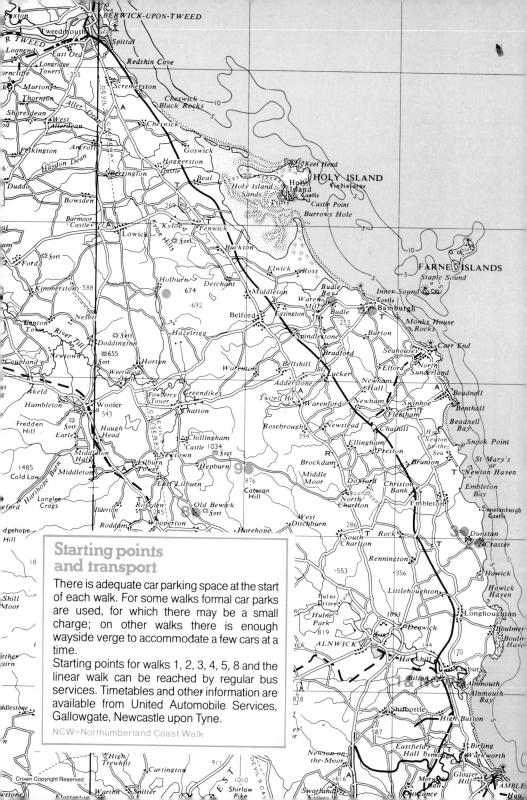

Starting points and transport

There is adequate car parking space at the start of each walk. For some walks formal car parks are used, for which there may be a small charge; on other walks there is enough wayside verge to accommodate a few cars at a time.

Starting points for walks 1, 2, 3, 4, 5, 8 and the linear walk can be reached by regular bus services. Timetables and other information are available from United Automobile Services, Gallowgate, Newcastle upon Tyne.

NCW—Northumberland Coast Walk

Introduction

The Northumberland coastline is an area of rare beauty. Under the Act of 1949 which saw the creation of National Parks, Areas of Outstanding Natural Beauty could also be designated. Since then 33 such areas in England and Wales, on the coast and inland, have been named and the stretch of Northumberland's coastline between Amble and Berwick is perhaps one of the finest. There is a requirement that the landscapes of both National Parks and Areas of Outstanding Natural Beauty should be protected, although for the latter no special provisions are made for recreation.

Additional recognition was given to the same stretch of coastline when in 1973 the Countryside Commission recommended its adoption as Heritage Coast. There are 35 of these stretches in the whole of England and Wales for which the Countryside Commission, with the local authorities for each area, has policies to provide for recreation as well as for landscape protection.

So, while Northumberland's coastline does not lie within the National Park it is, nevertheless, an important area for visitors exploring the county. The County Council is responsible for all public rights of way within the county as well as those within the Park; the paths used in this booklet, therefore, are maintained and signposted as part of the network of public rights of way in Northumberland.

The aim of this booklet is to provide both visitors and local people with walking routes and with interesting information regarding things to see on the way. Whilst we hope walkers will enjoy following the routes described, it is also hoped that they will accept the responsibility that goes with using the countryside, and keep the Country Code. This includes causing as little disturbance as possible to farm stock, keeping dogs under control, leaving gates as they find them, and not leaving litter to mar the enjoyment of the next walker.

Follow the Country Code

**Enjoy the countryside
and respect its life and work
Guard against all risk of fire
Fasten all gates
Keep your dog under close control
Keep to public paths across farmland
Use gates and stiles
to cross fences, hedges and walls
Leave livestock, crops and machinery alone
Take your litter home
Help to keep all water clean
Protect wild life, plants and trees
Take special care on country roads
Make no unnecessary noise**

Rights of way and using this booklet

As part of the programme involved in the production of this booklet all routes have been examined and signposts, stiles and waymarks provided where necessary.

In some places alternatives to the public rights of way have been agreed with the landowner to make walks more enjoyable. In these cases the routes are marked as permissive paths; these have no legal status and you can still use the public rights of way marked on the definitive map if you wish. The walks sometimes make use of the shoreline, the intertidal area for which no defined rights of way exist but open access is usually allowed. The same symbol as for permissive paths is used for these sections on the maps.

The maps have been drawn as simply as possible: contour lines are, for example, omitted, to avoid unnecessary visual confusion.

The route symbols are as follows:

Footpath	Bridleway ─ ─ ─ ─
Permissive path . ▬ .	Road ────────
Carriage Road Footpath ⊻ ⊻ ⊻ ⊻ ⊻ ⊻	
Carriage Road Bridleway ⋎ ⋎ ⋎ ⋎ ⋎ ⋎	

Interpretive notes are printed in normal weight type, route directions are given in bold type; GR refers to the Ordnance Survey grid reference system, details of which are printed on each of their 1:50000 series maps.

The first 9 walks in this booklet are circular routes, 6 on the coast and 3 on the range of hills inland. The last walk is linear, stretching 25 miles from Alnmouth Common in the south to Budle Bay in the north.

Enjoy your walk

Comfort is essential to the enjoyment of any walk so wear comfortable sensible shoes, or boots where a reading of the route notes might suggest it. Woollen socks, being more absorbent, are usually better to wear than those made from artificial fibres. Remember also that shores can be rocky as well as sandy and that it is all too easy to turn an ankle on these stones: footwear should give adequate support.

Walking may seem to be warm work but, especially at higher levels and on the coast it is possible to become chilled. Take a pullover, and remember a waterproof will keep out the wind as well as the rain.

Walks in this booklet have been calculated at roughly 1½ miles per hour to allow enough time for even the least experienced walker to complete the routes.

Hazards

Because many of these walks are on the coast there are one or two points that should be borne in mind when following the paths:

Tides

If the sea is particularly rough, or the tide is exceptionally high, keep well above the shoreline. In several places the text gives alternative routes if these circumstances are likely to arise. When the tide is out, remember that it is not always safe to walk straight across the sand immediately because the ground can still be too soft for safety, and there is a risk of being cut off by an incoming tide.

Weather

Weather can change very rapidly on the coast; bright sunshine can be very quickly obscured by thick fog, and this can extend some distance inland. If this should appear likely then think twice before setting out.

Cliffs

In one or two places the routes follow cliff tops, so don't go too near the edge.

Good stretches of coast attract golf courses. Three of these walks and parts of the linear walk go near or on golf courses. Remember that even the most experienced golfer sometimes slices a ball, so keep a weather eye open for such mishaps.

Dunstanburgh Castle - aerial view

About the Northumberland Coast

Many visitors to the Northumberland coast expect to find rugged cliffs or windswept marshes, conditions in keeping with the battle-scarred castles and the colonies of nesting seabirds for which the area is famed. Certainly the history and wildlife are quite exceptional, but conditions for walkers are far from hostile; the coastal landscape is exposed yet accessible and the footpaths and foreshore provide convenient walking routes with few hazards.

The coastline between Alnmouth and Holy Island is immensely varied, a succession of wide dune-backed bays intersected by rocky headlands and enhanced by estuaries, mudflats, rock shelves and islands. Inland, a coastal plain of good quality farmland leads to a ridge of high sandstone moorland, among the least visited in the county and of considerable beauty.

In many ways this corner of Northumberland has been unexplored; as a unit it has been strongly influenced by man, but if anything this influence has diminished through the centuries. The interface between land and sea was once busily exploited for quarry-stone, agricultural fertiliser and seafood, but these traditions have dwindled to such an extent that their effect on the landscape is hardly visible. What is left is picturesque rather than functional, and this applies also to the most dramatic remnants of past glory – the great castles of Bamburgh and Dunstanburgh, the Priory and Castle of Lindisfarne and the pele towers and the

monastic ruins built when the county was a
military and religious power base.

The agricultural land, mostly arable but retaining
a significant element of its cattle-rearing
tradition, has kept its pastoral appearance
despite the changes imposed by modern
technology. Fields are still of moderate size,
bounded in most cases by hedges rather than
fences or walls, and although most farm
buildings have been modernised they still look
part of the original picture – discrete corners of a
brightly coloured patchwork. The dark moorland
between Eglingham and Belford was once
inhabited too, by Bronze Age and Iron Age
communities who left a bewildering inheritance
of cairns, cists and hill forts. After their demise
and the eventual removal of any forest cover the
moors became a heather-clad wilderness,
protected for grouse and sheep-rearing by the
great estates.

The Coastal Walks

The first 6 walks of this booklet follow circular
routes incorporating significant sections of the
coast. They include attractive areas of farmland
and heath and, in some cases, fishing villages
and settlements. Since the interpretive
information about wildlife and history has to
relate to visible features, many interesting
items, for example in the intertidal zone, have
had to be omitted. An identification book relating
to life in rock pools is definitely worth carrying;
so is a plastic bag for the shellfish, fossils and
pebbles that are certain to be picked up along
the way.

1 Alnmouth - Lesbury ;
return via Foxton Hall and Alnmouth Beach

4 miles, about 2½ hours. Not conventionally beautiful since it contains a close look at mudflats, but these places are so unusual in Northumberland that the walk is almost unique. Two very old settlements, an attractive river and a fine stretch of beach complete the route.

Leave cars on Alnmouth Common – to the north-east of the town (signposted as the main car park along the Wynd, first left as you turn into the town and fork left after 100 yards (91m)). Park next to the old lifeboat station, beyond the golf course. There may be a small car parking charge.

Looking out to sea, the bay sweeps round to the right towards Hauxley Point. About a mile out from Hauxley and five miles from Alnmouth is Coquet Island, its white lighthouse showing clearly on its western side. Quite a small island,

only 16 acres (6.5 hectares) in total and not as well known as the Farnes or Holy Island to the north. It is, however, of some historical interest having housed Benedictine monks in the 7th century, and being the site of a minor skirmish during the English Civil War. It is a bird reserve now, famous for its nesting terns. Common and arctic are the most frequent types, but unless seen at close quarters they are impossible to tell apart. Birdwatchers, not always known for their sense of humour, often call them comic terns and leave it at that. Coquet Island is also the breeding head-quarters of the roseate tern, a beautiful

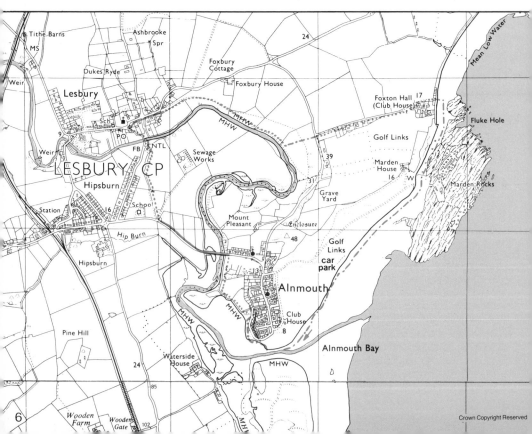

Tidal section of the River Aln, looking towards Lesbury

creature with long tail streamers and a rose-flush to its plumage. Its world-wide range has been decreasing for some time and it could be heading for total extinction.

Walk right, towards the mouth of the Aln, keeping at first to the dune track but eventually, at any convenient place, bearing left onto the beach.

The well-trodden dunes have an assortment of colourful plants. Ragwort is probably the most obvious, bright yellow and a foot or so tall. It is poisonous to cattle but during July and August is usually covered with caterpillars of the cinnabar moth. These actually use the toxin to defend themselves against birds, showing by their orange and black stripes that they are thoroughly distasteful. Cinnabars were once exported to New Zealand in an unsuccessful attempt to control the spread of ragwort in that country. One of the theories to account for the failure was that the local birds hadn't learnt the colour coding.

Alnmouth, across the common to the right, grew from humble beginnings to be one of the most important harbours in medieval Northumberland. Corn became its major commodity, stored in the tall warehouses that now serve as hotels and private dwellings.

Continue along the high tide mark. Bear right into the mouth of the estuary, opposite a large green mound on the other side of the river.

Prior to its growth as a grain harbour Alnmouth was comparatively obscure, but stood at a strategic point between the diocese of Hexham and Lindisfarne. St. Cuthbert was probably here in 684 when he was elected Bishop of Hexham, only to turn that see down in favour of his beloved Lindisfarne. The site of this synod was almost certainly the green hill across the Aln, described by Bede as 'Twyford', the place of two fords, and subsequently the location of St. Waleric's Chapel. Church Hill, as it is now called, was once attached to the rest of the town, but the river changed course in 1806, severing Alnmouth from its only substantial legend.

Follow the line of buildings to the right of the muddy estuary. (Along the tide-line if dry, or if the tide is high by climbing the steps on the right and walking left along the road.)

The area of 'slake' or salt-marsh is covered with *Spartina* grass. Purslane and sea aster (which looks very like michaelmas daisy) are quite common too – all thriving in the grey mud.

This leads you to a small children's playground; go through this onto a road called Garden Terrace, and turn left. After only 5 yards (4m) turn left again through a narrow stile which brings you back into view of the estuary. Continue along this path, with a short wall to your left. (If the alternative route has been taken continue past the beached boats between the trees, and at the 'Garden Terrace' sign turn left through a narrow stile between a 5-bar gate and the electricity sub-station.)

The creeks and backwaters attract wading birds like greenshank and bar-tailed godwit, especially in the late summer and autumn when they are migrating south. Many breed in the Arctic and overwinter in Africa.

Painted Lady Butterfly on Thistle

The path leads to Duchess's Bridge. Go up the steps, over the road and turn left over the footway. Keep on the right-hand side of the road as it bears right. Where it bends to the left, about 100 yards (91m) before the school, look for an old wicket gate (right). This is just after the entrance to the local cricket ground. Go through the wicket and over the field, keeping the hedge to your right.

If the thistles are in flower, try smelling them. Surprisingly, it is the smaller creeping thistle that has the attractive scent; the larger spear thistle has virtually none.

Continue to the end of the field, then round to the right of a very old hawthorn hedge (now 20 feet (7m) tall). Through a wicket gate, keep the fence on your right until, about 80 yards (73m) after the end of the houses, the path bears left to a road. Turn right along the road, which leads over a footbridge.

The Aln is very beautiful here: a typical 'middle reach', fast flowing and sandy, with water crowfoot (an aquatic type of buttercup) waving in the current. Alders and willows line the banks.

The path turns left before bearing right into the village of Lesbury.

Lesbury was once as important as Alnwick or Alnmouth, but whilst they expanded it remained much the same size. The name is derived from the Old English 'laece' and 'burg' i.e. the home of the leech or physician.

Turn right opposite the church and walk along the main street. Continue up the hill, having passed the turn to R.A.F. Boulmer on the left. 100 yards (91m) after the junction, the road bears left; look for a footpath between 2 houses to the right. Turn into this then go through a small gate which opens out into a field.

Old ridge and furrow markings show that the pasture has been under cultivation for

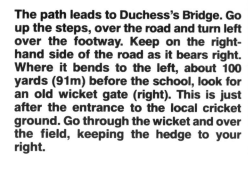

River Aln from the bridge at Lesbury

hundreds of years, though cattle stealing was popular in the area and the pasture may have been abandoned during Norman times.

Bear right, down to the river. Continue alongside the river through another 2 fields.

The Aln has changed completely here; it is now tidal and salt water has altered the whole ecology. The green waterweed is called *Enteromorpha* – shaped like an unravelled intestine and bright green in colour. The Japanese are supposed to eat it, although *Porphyra* (equally unappetising) is the species at the centre of the massive Japanese seaweed industry.

Two birds seem particularly associated with this area. Herons hunt the shallows at dawn and dusk, and shelducks, distinctive in their bright pied plumage, can often be seen in small groups loafing about on the banks. Both have a reputation for being totally inedible. W.H. Hudson, the classic nature writer, once dedicated a whole chapter to 'The Heron as a Table Bird'. The story he relates is of a farmer who had made his sisters cook a heron for him and serve it as Sunday dinner. The sisters were far too sensible to take a bite themselves but watched with interest as their brother took a generous mouthful, changed colour and disappeared from the table in a hurry. He was not seen until the following evening and the subject was never raised again.

At the telegraph poles turn left, keeping the line of the poles slightly to your left as you climb the steep (but short) hillside. This leads to a road.

Looking back, there are good views of Alnwick Moor and the Cheviot Hills.

Go straight across the road and down the drive signposted 'Alnmouth Golf Club'.

Prime arable land lies to the left and secluded detached houses to the right. The hedgerow is interesting, however, and includes a range of spring flowers such as violet and celandine. The latter was once used medicinally. Unlike bladderwort and liverwort, however, its application is no longer commemorated in its name; it used to be called pilewort.

At Foxton Hall (the Golf Club), take the path to the left of the Members' Car Park sign, which bears right and down the bramble-lined path to the sea. Turn right on the beach.

There is a wide pebble-and-sand bay to the north; walking south around the front of the Hall takes you past the Fluke Hole (a gap in the rocks visible at low tide) and alongside Marden Rocks. Close to the high water mark is a shelf of shale and limestone, dipping into the sea and resembling a flagged pavement.

Alnmouth Bay

It is possible to return to the car park by walking along the crest of the grassy ridge to the right, but the beach provides a much more enjoyable route.

The huge concrete blocks are part of the coastal defences put up during the Second World War: a reminder of an invasion that never happened. This is not to say that Alnmouth Bay has avoided any naval excitement. In 1744 two ships, the *Thames and Margaret* out of Sunderland, and a Berwick brigantine laden with corn, were captured by a privateer following a 5 hour engagement. 27 people were killed. Years later, in 1779, the American ship *Ranger* fired a 28lb cannon-ball at the old church but missed. John Paul Jones, its captain, obviously considered it an adequate gesture and departed without more ado. The cannon-ball bounced its way inland and demolished the gable-end of a farm about a mile to the south-west.

Continue along the tideline, past the breakwaters, and to the car park beyond the old lifeboat station.

2 Craster - Howick ;
return via Cullernose Point

4½ miles, about 3 hours. The outward route makes its way across varied pasture and arable land towards the richly wooded estate of Howick Hall. The return follows the coastal footpath, above some of the finest rocky shores in the county.

Park at the car park, on the right as you enter the village. There may be a small charge.

The car park is within the shell of the old Craster Quarry, famous for its whinstone; uneconomic by the late 1930s, it was reopened briefly during the Second World War. The quarried stone, dark grey and very hard-wearing, was ideal for metalling roads but was unsuitable for building as it could not be worked or faced easily. It was carried by an overhead cableway down to the harbour, from whence it found its way to cities on the east coast as far south as London.

Once its active life had finished the quarry was quickly colonised by trees and bushes, which in turn attracted insects and birds. The area is now a nature reserve of the Northumberland Wildlife Trust, dedicated to the memory of Dr Lawrence Arnold.

Behind the Wildlife Trust displays, a path leads right, through an area of scrub and thorny woodland.

Knapweed, elder and hawthorn provide food for finches and buntings; the abundance of insects and the fresh water account for all the warblers, which arrive from Africa in April and May and stay to raise 1 or 2 broods before starting the return journey in September. A precarious life! In 1969 only a quarter of the whole British population of whitethroats survived the flight north, probably because they failed to find enough food in the 'fuelling-up' stage south of the Sahara. Blackcaps, chiffchaffs and willow-warblers, all present here at Craster, suffer from the same succession of hardships. In the space of 2-3 months they have to stake out a territory, sing to defend it, attract a mate and raise a family, and then get themselves into shape for the journey south.

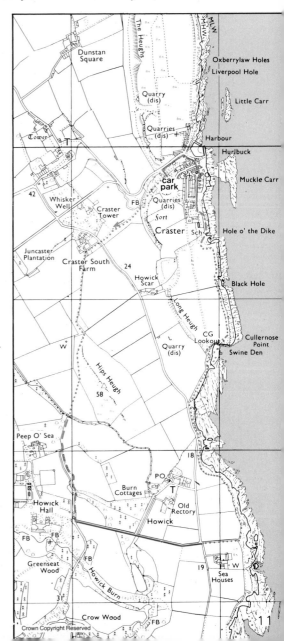

Continue along the path with the old quarry face – now wooded – on the left. Keep to the bottom path, bearing left at the first junction but right at the second, which leads out onto an open field. Walk straight up the field with Craster South Farm ahead.

This is very old pasture land; the ridge and furrow marks to the left of the path run in a different direction to those on the right, suggesting an Anglo-Saxon field system.

To the right as you approach the gate is Craster Tower, built before 1415 and inhabited by the family who gave their name to both home and village. The name is derived from 'Craucestr,' i.e. the old fort inhabited by crows. Rooks (which were once called crows) still nest in the trees that screen the tower.

The Crasters were successful soldiers. Two were with Sir John Grey at the Battle of Agincourt, and others held such positions as Bailiff of Bamburgh, Constable of Dunstanburgh and Governor of Morpeth Castle during the 16th and 17th centuries.

Go through the gate, across the road and up the side-road towards Craster South Farm. Carry straight on to the right of the terrace of cottages. The path then leads half left through a gate and into the corner of a field. Continue along the edge of the field.

Hips Heugh

Hares are quite numerous in these open fields, perhaps because there is plenty of stubble and they can find quiet grassy places away from farm dogs and men with guns. Alternatively, it could be that Celtic magic is still practised in the nearby villages, since witches turn themselves into hares to avoid recognition.

Through an old gate, follow the path as it gradually gains height towards Hips Heugh, the craggy hilltop a little way ahead.

The sea is partly hidden by a long whinstone ridge, cut here and there by meltwater channels formed during the Ice Age.

Inland to the right (west) is Craster West Farm; on a clear day the Cheviot Hills will be visible about 20 miles beyond.

The footpath bears left as the field narrows, and the old hawthorn hedge is replaced by a stone wall.

The wall is plastered with what might look like dabs of whitewash. In fact it is a lichen called *Lecanora* which grows well in the clean salty air. It is difficult to believe that lichens are living plants at all, but they are well suited to the conditions and are a highly specialised team of algae and fungi working together within an organised framework.

Ploughed field and oak/elm woodland, near Peep O'Sea farm.

Go over the stile at the end of the field. Bear right below the face of Hips Heugh.

Dolerite, of which these crags are formed, produces some fine columns and pillars. Fingal's Cave is of the same type of material, and so is the Giant's Causeway in Ireland. Trees and bushes do well in the cracks and fissures because they can gain a firm grip, and because erosion is slow.

Gorse and ivy are the most common shrubs here, and foxgloves (known as deadmen's bells) thrive on the scree below.

The footpath continues alongside the wall to the right. 100 yards (91m) past the 2 sycamore trees there is a gate through the wall, with a stile alongside it. Go over the stile and across the field, bearing slightly to the left to bring you to a 5-bar gate with tall elms to its right.

The small burn in front of the gate marks the parish boundary between Longhoughton and Craster. Natural features were used to define such boundaries and were often reinforced with ridges or hedges. The burn here is lined with ash, elm and hawthorn, probably the remains of an ancient enclosure.

Go through the gate and along the right-hand side of the field, with Peep O'Sea Farm visible through the trees to the right.

The belt of damp woodland contains some majestic trees, especially ash, sweet chestnut and oak. The ground is covered in places by dog's mercury, an indicator of old woodland and known in some places as 'boggart posy' – boggart being a nasty bogy or ghost. The plant is 'dangerously purgative', so perhaps its victims might be excused for haunting woods in a particularly unhappy state.

Through another gate, and the edge of the wood bears slightly left, then sharply right, into the corner of the field. In the dip there is a track cutting the belt of trees and leading up to a gate. Go through this and continue up the track.

There is a large ash stump on the right just after the gate. The holes in the rotting wood show how important these sites are for insects – especially beetles, bees and solitary wasps.

Continue over the brow of a hill and through another gate onto a metalled track which follows a tall stone wall down to a road.

To the right is the entrance to Howick Hall, screened by trees. The present Hall was built in 1782 by Sir Henry Grey, but the credit for the wooded setting must go to the second Earl Grey who enlarged the Hall in 1812 and planted thousands of saplings to improve landscaping. His son, writing in the mid-19th century, recalled with touching nostalgia the walks that the family used to take around their estate. 'It is difficult to exaggerate the beauty and variety of the sea coast and views that met you at every turn of the sea walk.' The coast is still beautiful of course, but when an old man looks back on his youth he remembers much more than just the scenery.

Turn left down the road, along the pavement on the left-hand side.

The earth-banks on the road verges indicate that this is an ancient avenue, and the beech and elm trees are impressively gnarled and thick-rooted.

Continue past the turning to Howick village. After 100 yards (91m) the old rectory, shrouded in trees, is visible on the left. Continue over the crest of the hill, and when the road turns sharp left, take the footpath that goes straight towards the sea. It is signposted 'Coastal Path. Craster 2.'

The bushes on the left are sea buckthorn and elder. The former has very beautiful orange berries in the autumn, and very sharp thorns. Sea Houses, the group of buildings to the right,

includes a good example of a 'gin-gan': a round structure in which a horse or donkey was used to drive farm machinery.

Through the gate at the end of the track, turn left along the coastal footpath.

The sandy bay is enclosed by shallow sandstone cliffs and blocks, cross-bedded and heavily weathered. If the tide is out, explore the seaward side and you may discover the Rumbling Kern – an enclosed chasm or cave through which the sea gurgles, making a sound like a giant with indigestion.

Take the path to the left, above the cliff-top cottage.

Victorians were very keen on water; this bathing house was built for the Grey family so that they could enjoy a dip whilst retaining the necessary convenience of a sturdy cottage. Tents were erected close to the shore to facilitate a dash for cover once they had finished their swim. The building is now a holiday home.

The path continues above the cliffs of sandstone and shale and gradually bears left to reveal a fine view of the rocky coast to the north. The sandstone disappears very suddenly, replaced across a fault-line by 'six-yard limestone', grey in colour and distorted into all sorts of shapes. The geology is very confusing, and a hotch-potch of small seams and metamorphosed sediments occur here.

The path meets the Craster road and runs parallel with it for a while, cutting through blackthorn scrub as it bears right towards Cullernose Point.

A British submarine ran aground here on Armistice night, 1918. Despite all attempts to salvage her she had to be blown up, but not before everything of value had been stripped from her.

The large gull-grey birds that soar stiff-winged along the cliff edges are not gulls at all, but fulmars, the nearest thing to albatrosses that we have. They nest all along this coast.

Continue north-east, along the gravelled path that descends towards Cullernose.

Sandstone and shale, sculpted by the sea, south of Cullernose. ▷

The Bathing House, north-east of Seahouses Farm

Cullernose is an austere face of dolerite, with fulmars in residence for most of the year, but not necessarily the same birds all the time and not always looking for nesting sites. It often seems they just want somewhere to sit to be able to cackle at each other.

Beneath the cliff is Swine Den – a beach of well-rounded whinstone boulders.

Climb the path onto the ridge of Long Heugh. Through the gate, turn right towards the coastguard hut. Keep left of the fence line and cut-off the corner (of Cullernose Point) by turning left at the hut. This brings you back onto the coastal path, though the short-cropped turf makes it difficult to see its actual line.

Continue north, through another wicket gate alongside a 5-bar gate.

The shelf of dolerite, dipping into the sea, is bitten into by a chasm called the Black Hole. Not *that* sort of black hole, but an apt description for the splash zone of black lichen, called *Verrucaria,* which covers the lower section of the rocks. The orange lichen above the splash zone is *Xanthoria* (the X is pronounced like a Z) – one of the few species identifiable at a range of more than a centimetre.

To the north, Dunstanburgh Castle will now dominate the skyline above Craster village. Muckle Carr, an outcrop of limestone just out of Craster harbour, may be submerged if the tide is in; the twin navigation aids of Little Carr will be visible a little way to the north.

A short distance further on, the path abruptly turns left and then bears right to regain the coastline. Over a stile, with the village school to the left, continue until you reach the football field – at which point cut across left onto a road. Go on to the end of the road, then turn right and left and into the centre of Craster.

The village may have closed its quarries and lost most of its fishing tradition, but it is still famous for its kippers. Buy some if they are in season (June – September). If not, look at the tidy little harbour and imagine what it must have been like 70 years ago – full of dust from the whinstone quarrying, and the noise and bustle of a community at work.

Take the road inland, left around the inshore lifeboat station. After 200 yards (182m) the car park is on the left.

3 Dunstan Steads - Craster ; return via Dunstan Square

4½ miles, about 3 hours. An easy grassland walk, dominated by the sea and the skeletal remains of Dunstanburgh Castle. Inland, gorse-covered heughs and well maintained farmland provide an alternative view of the coastal landscape.

Park just down the road from Dunstan Steads Farm, on the verge to the right of the road. Walk down to the road end and through the gate leading to the dunes and sea. Go straight across the golf course towards the gap in the dune ridge.

Sand dunes accumulate a very distinctive set of plants, some small and insignificant, others quite large and gaudy. From June until August, bloody cranesbill covers the pathside with its saucer-shaped flowers. The name refers to its colour, though it is sometimes called blood-red cranesbill in a prissy attempt to make flower books less shocking. The scrambling thorn bushes, spiky and fine-leaved, are of burnet rose, one of the most compact of all the wild roses with deep cream flowers and an indescribably beautiful scent.

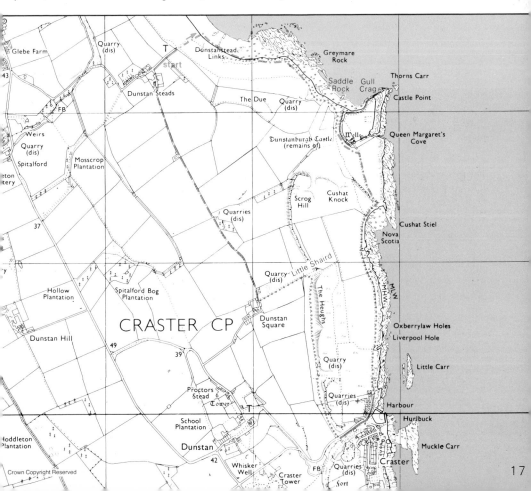

17

Dunstanburgh and Gull Crag, from Saddle Rock

At the beach, turn right.

Embleton Bay, with Dunstanburgh to the south, is as pretty as a post-card; fortunately it has escaped the fate of many other picturesque beaches. Looking back to the north, the small huts and chalets on Newton Point are a reminder of what the bay might be like if it were in the south of England.

Continue on the high-tide mark until the sand gives way to rounded boulders, at which point climb the grassy dune ridge and walk along the path.

The boulders are of grey dolerite – pieces of Whin Sill that have fallen into the sea and been clipped and polished until they are smooth. As the path bears right, to the south of the bay and before the cliff and castle are reached, there is a distinctive outcrop of limestone called Saddle Rock. It is contorted like a buckled sandwich cake and its various layers dip down into the sea, giving way to a bed of even larger dolerite boulders, too big and heavy for the sea to lift – yet.

The path leads through a wicket gate and leaves the dunes and golf course behind as it approaches the cliffs and castle.

The dark cliff face is called Gull Crag and is plastered with the nests and droppings of kittiwakes – small ocean-going gulls that take over the place during the summer months. Among the hordes of kittiwakes there are a few fulmars, guillemots and shag, though only the fulmars remain on the ledges after September. Dolerite forms the top 50 feet (15m) of Gull Crag – the other 60 or 70 feet (18 or 21m, depending on the tide), are of sandstone and shale.

Follow the path round to the right, bearing left uphill as far as the keep (main entrance) of the castle.

To many people Dunstanburgh is the finest of the local castles, superbly sited, ruinous and hardly altered since Tudor times.
In 1538 Henry VIII was sent a report from his commissioners which described the castle as 'a very reuynus howsse and of smaylle strengthe', and so it remained, providing roofing lead and building stone for whatever projects were under way in the area.
Dunstanburgh was started in 1313 by Thomas, second Earl of Lancaster, and was completed in about 1316. Thomas was executed by Edward II only 6 years later, following the Battle of Boroughbridge, and it was left to John of Gaunt

to bring the castle up to fighting trim for the Border Wars of the 1380s. Following this it was an important Lancastrian stronghold throughout the Wars of the Roses but was allowed to fall into decay after 1470.

Perhaps the centuries of dereliction are responsible for the legends that hover around the place. The most famous is of Sir Guy the Seeker, who took refuge in the castle during a storm; he was visited by a 'ghastly wight' (ghost) who led him to a beautiful maiden in a crystal tomb, bewitched and guarded by 100 sleeping knights. He was offered the choice of a sword or a horn to break the spell. Oddly enough (considering the sleeping knights) he chose the horn and blew it lustily. It was the wrong choice of course, and his spirit still walks the ruins trying to find the stairs to the maiden's chamber.

From the castle, walk south down the grassy hillside and alongside the small sandy bay called Nova Scotia.

A Polish trawler came aground here one foggy morning in July 1958. If the tide is out the wreck can still be seen. To the right is a marshy piece of ground that was once a sea-filled ditch around the castle. It was also a harbour, and it was here in 1514 that Thomas Beverley (described as 'an honest, sad and secret person') found the fleet of Henry VIII's warships that had put out from Hull some 3 weeks before, bound for the Firth of Forth. Why they hid themselves at Dunstanburgh is something of a mystery.

On the other side of the bay, continue south towards Craster.

To the left is a shelf of dolerite, dipping down to the sea and containing several rock pools. These are not as dramatic as on other sections of the coast, but are quite accessible. Those closest to the sea are the most interesting, harbouring beadlet anemones, dog whelks and periwinkles.

Just before the village of Craster, the twin markers on the Little Carr can be seen to the left. These were constructed as navigation aids to the fishing fleet working out of Craster. A hundred years ago there were 27 cobles in the fleet; today there are 4 or 5.

Into Craster village, the path ends at a gate. A road leads on, past the little harbour.

The harbour was constructed in 1906 by the Craster family, as a memorial to Captain Craster, killed in India on the Tibetan expedition of 1904. The strange concrete block at the end of the south pier is all that remains of a tall hopper into which whinstone chips were deposited by an overhead cableway leading from the quarries. Operations ceased before the Second World War, although one quarry reopened for part of it.

20

Take the main road to the right, out of the village.

The house on the right, with the eccentric boat-bedecked entrance is called 'The Choughs', named after an attractive bird of the crow family but a species never found on these shores.

Opposite the car park, take the footpath right, marked 'Dunstan Square 1m'.

This leads through a hawthorn and briar thicket and opens out to a grassy path with whinstone crags to the right. Bluebells form a thick band at their base; these are woodland plants by inclination, demanding sunshine in the spring and shade during the summer. In this situation, bracken provides the necessary cover, however, and the bluebells are hidden from view for all but a month or so each spring.

After a wicket gate continue north along this path, with the whinstone heugh to the right and a tall hawthorn hedge to the left.

The top and upper sides of the heugh are covered with gorse; during warm sunny days the flowers give off a heavy coconut-scented fug and are alive with bees. Hawthorn bushes grow better nearer the base and these are used by insect-eating birds, particularly the willow warbler which delivers a subtle descending song, full of uncertainty but very much a sound of summer. For the rest of the year the harsh rattle of the wren is the only likely bird song.

At the end of the tall hedge with Little Shaird (the gap in the whinstone heugh) to the right, go through the wicket gate and turn left.

Dunstan Square is visible at the top of the hill. A little to the left and about half a mile beyond is Proctors Stead, once called Dunstan Hall and a possible birthplace of Duns Scotus, the medieval scholar. However, he is generally thought to have come from Duns in Scotland. The old Pele Tower was built at the same time as Dunstanburgh Castle, though the lower part is much older.

After another gate, continue up to Dunstan Square. At the farm, turn right

along the bridleway marked 'Dunstan Steads', through a gate and along the concrete trackway.

Dunstanburgh Castle is again visible, this time as a disembodied set of towers above Scrog Hill to the right.

At a cattle grid, the wall changes from the right side of the path to the left. Continue north, past the small pine plantation.

There is a pill-box to the left and an old lime-kiln to the right. Both look strangely out of place, although the kiln would have been very important for the production of slaked lime, an early agricultural fertilizer.

Over another road grid, the path leads towards Dunstan Steads.

The concrete structure on the left is a silage pit. In the spring it will probably be empty, but when the grass crop has been cut it will be full and covered with black plastic – probably weighted down with old car tyres. Silage is fermented grass, and air has to be kept out of the mixture to make sure that the right bacteria get to work. It is fed to cattle during the winter, and on many farms it has replaced the traditional hay crop because its production is not so dependent on the weather.
Unfortunately, silage is cut a little earlier than hay, and wild flowers do not have a chance to produce seed in the same way as they do in hayfields. This makes grass fields very dull but more productive.

Go through Dunstan Steads Farm (keeping to the path), turn right at the road and back to the starting point.

Kittiwake,

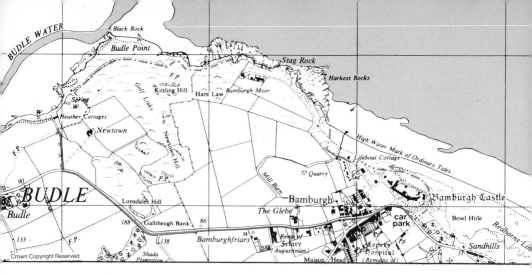

4 Bamburgh - Budle Point ; return via Newtown Farm and Bamburghfriars

4 miles, about 2¾ hours. A castle, a coast, dunes and whinstone crags, finishing with rich arable fields and an historic village.

Leave cars in the main car park, opposite the castle, and cross the road to take a path up to the right of the castle.

Huge square structures do not blend well into a landscape. When castles were first invented they must have brooded over things in the same way that nuclear power stations do today. Bamburgh is so big and so solid on its dolerite foundations that to be this close to it can be disquieting. Its pedigree, however, is one of the best in Britain. Ida, first of the Northumbrian kings, had the first significant fortification built in 547. In those days it only had a hedge around it (the first one in Britain ever documented) and was called 'Dinguvaroy', but the Celts in the district had no answer to the charisma or power of the Angle invader (they called him 'Flamebearer') and his castle became the centrepiece of a respectable kingdom. Later, his grandson, Ethelfrith (a fine name!) gave it to his queen, Bebba, so it became 'Bebbanburgh' during the 7th century. After this it is linked with some of the most significant events in English history. The Danes pillaged it on several occasions, but it was reconstructed each time and was of great

strategic importance to the Normans. Its end as a great castle came during the Wars of the Roses in the 15th century; the use of gunpowder had made castles vulnerable at last and Bamburgh was the first in England to fall as a result of artillery bombardment. Despite some restoration, it gradually fell derelict and it was only at the turn of the present century that it was extensively rebuilt.

In front of the castle, take the narrow path that descends to the right of the wooden fence, just across the metalled road from the castle entrance.

Hemlock seems to grow particularly well here; a tall member of the 'umbellifer' family of plants with umbrella-shaped flower heads and a red-freckled base. During the winter the bleached stem skeletons often stand 6 or 7 feet (about 2m) tall, brittle and less deadly. Hemlock was used to poison Socrates and has long had an evil reputation.

Follow the fence-line at the bottom of the bank, still bearing left. Keep to this path and make for the far corner (north corner) of the castle rock.

Redbarns Links – the dunes to the right – are very dramatic, fixed in place by a carpet of marram grass. In the foreground is a great bowl of blown sand, showing why marram is so important in the prevention of windblow.

The path turns left after passing beneath a whinstone cliff, then, after some castle ruins to the left it bears right to meet a road at Lifeboat Cottage. Continue along the road to the right, over the Mill Burn and to the crown of the next hill, at which point turn right across the dunes to the high water mark. Turn left and make your way towards Harkess Rocks.

The view back towards the castle is a classic, appearing on all sorts of pictures and posters. These never seem to include the bathing huts and chalets, but the vista is still breathtaking – especially on a falling tide with the castle shining off the sands. Harkess Rocks are part of the Whin Sill, but at this point there are fragments of sandstone and shale mixed into the dark grey dolerite. The Sill was formed by lava being pushed up between sediments, and the high temperatures and pressures involved must have melted and shattered many of the adjacent rocks. These mixed into a kind of lumpy soup before cooling into their present state.

If the tide is out, walk along the rocks beneath the grass bank. If the sea is in an ugly mood, however, climb the bank and continue west along the roadside.

This can be a very exposed section of coast and there have been many shipwrecks. In 1472 James Kennedy, bishop of St. Andrews and grandson of Robert III of Scotland, lost a fortune in the shape of the *St. Salvador* – carrying a cargo of 'rich merchandise' from Flanders. According to the Annals of Scotland most of the crew were drowned 'except some few that saved their lieves in the ships boate, amonest quhom was the abbot of St. Columbane'. It says much for the times that the abbot was immediately imprisioned until an £80 ransom had been paid, and the 'merchandise' probably found its way into half the houses of Bamburgh.

Stop at the lighthouse.

Just seaward of the lighthouse is Stag Rock, named after the white stag painted onto a shelf of dolerite and retouched whenever the lighthouse gets a fresh coat of paint. It is a famous seawatching point for birdwatchers, particularly when north-easterly gales are blowing. A great many seabirds such as gannets and skuas fly along this coast, and rough or misty conditions can bring them close in to hug the shoreline. Seawatching is sometimes spectacular, often exciting but invariably uncomfortable.

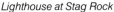
Lighthouse at Stag Rock

Bear left of the lighthouse, and along the path at the base of the grassy bank, above the rocks. This takes you down to a small sandy bay. Walk along the shore as far as the lifebuoy, at which point take a path, left, up to the top of the bank and bear right along the edge of the golf course. The path leads through the remains of an old drystone wall.

To the left is Kittling Hill, a disused quarry colonised by fulmars. Crossleaved heath (known locally as she-heather) covers its flanks but the north-facing quarry wall has remained bare. Fulmar droppings are perhaps responsible for the growth of elder bushes on the lower crags.

Surprisingly, golf courses often provide good habitats for wildlife, particularly when they are situated close to the sea. The greens are heavily cut and weeded, but the roughs always hide interesting plants and insects. The ground here is slightly acidic: gorse and bell-heather are visible most of the year, whilst harebell and tormentil are usually noticed in the late summer when the flowers are at their best. Drinker moth caterpillars are quite common in the spring and early summer; they are very large and unusually hairy and sit about on grass stems for much of the time. Cuckoos are the only birds that will eat them with any relish – but cuckoos are odd birds in other ways too.

The path leads to the start of a wide stony track (of whinstone chips), which continues north-west, around Budle Point.

The track is all that remains of the old tramway which was used to transport whinstone boulders from the quarry down to the quay.

Ross Back Sands stretches away in a graceful curve beyond Budle Point. It is one of the least spoilt beaches in Britain, partly because it is inaccessible and partly because on windy days there is no shelter and any exposed skin is quickly sand-blasted to a deep golden tan – or a painful pink! The stretch of sea just out from the beach is called Skate Road and is attractive to many waterfowl – grebes, divers and mergansers in particular, all searching for fish in the shallow waters.

Holy Island, beyond Old Law (the dune island at the very end of Ross Back Sands), often looks as if it is just an extension of Ross Links. It is less than 5 miles away, but on misty days it can seem very much further.

A Second World War gun emplacement looks out at the head of Budle Bay, over the old quay and towards what used to be called the German Ocean.

Take the pathway left around the gun emplacement, then sharp left up onto the golf links. Go round to the right of

St. Aidan's Church, Bamburgh

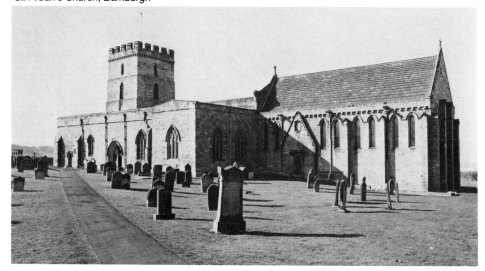

Bamburgh Castle, from the south

the greens, then right along a wide track to a gateway. This leads out onto a metalled road with caravans to the right. Bear left along the road.

Newtown Farm, to the left, is festooned with wind-sails to generate electricity: there are few completely windless days in the year!

The road leads down to a gate, with caravans and Heather Cottages to the right. Turn left, and continue uphill to a gate. Go through this and onto the main road, at which turn left. Keep to the wide verge on the left side of the road and continue over the brow of the hill.

The view of Bamburgh village and castle is excellent from this point. The areas of gorse and elder on the hillsides, particularly on Newtown Hill across the field on the left, past Galliheugh Bank, are full of birds and animals. Roe deer hide among the bracken and during the autumn and winter short-eared owls hunt for voles on the open slopes.

Continue along the road verge towards Bamburgh.

The first farm on the right (The Friars) is sited next to the ruins of a Dominican Friary. The area is more famous for its Augustinian associations, however, and there are many references to them in the history of the church and castle. Few stones remain today to bear witness to their work.

Further into the village, on the right, past several newer dwellings that have made use of ancient walls and foundations, is the Grace Darling Museum. If open it is well worth a visit since it contains the coble (fishing boat) in which Grace and her father went to the rescue of men from the *Forfarshire,* wrecked on the Farnes' Harcar Rocks in 1838. The event has been greatly romanticised, and many of the contemporary paintings show the tiny coble amid mountainous seas. A small painting in the museum by H.O. Hall – the heroine's great-great-nephew – probably gives a much more accurate view of the event and does not diminish the bravery or courage involved.

Across the road is St. Aidan's Church, where Grace Darling is buried. She died aged 26, only 4 years after the rescue had made her a reluctant celebrity in Victorian England. The church is named after a far-sighted monk from Iona sent at the request of King (later Saint) Oswald to convert the Northumbrians after a previous missionary had proved too severe for the local temperament. Aidan succeeded in spectacular fashion and established a wooden church on the present site, but nothing remains of this except (possibly) a beam over the baptistry which may have stood on the outer shell of the original church. It is said that Aidan was propped up against this beam when he died, and that subsequent fires burnt down the rest of the building but failed, miraculously, to damage the beam.

Carry on down the road and into the village centre, and from there on to the car park.

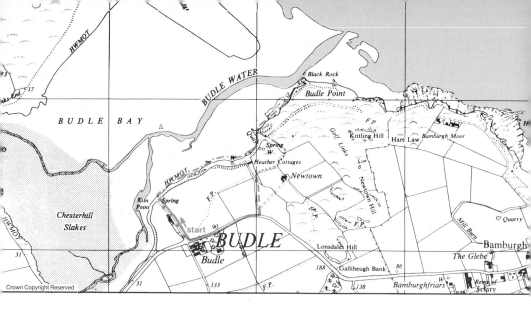

5 Budle - Budle Point ;
return via Heather Cottages

2 miles, about 1½ hours. A very short walk, but the view of the bay and its wildlife make it dramatic in both winter and summer.

Park at Budle on the verge close to the footpath notice, on the north-east side of the cross-road. Walk down the track towards the bay, going through the gate with cottages to the left.

Swallows and sand martins nest close by, and in the summer and autumn they often sit on the telephone wires above the trackway. Browning wrote about their autumn congregations:

> The swallow has set her six young on
> the rail, and looks seaward.

This was a considerable advance on the thinking of 100 years earlier, when Thomson had written of swallows:

> rejoicing once,
> Ere to their wintry slumbers they retire.

Nobody in the 18th century believed that swallows migrated to another country; the theory was that they dived into ponds and hibernated in the mud.
To the right, at the end of the track, is a lime kiln.

On a clear day the more extensive set of kilns on Holy Island will be visible to the north-east, a little to the right of the castle. Even remote farming communities needed lime, and it was much cheaper to do the job locally, bringing both coal and limestone from nearby pits and quarries.

At the end of the track, stop at the National Nature Reserve notice board.

The area of Lindisfarne National Nature Reserve extends north beyond Holy Island, and represents one of the best intertidal habitats in the whole country. During the winter the area of Chesterhill Slakes — the muddy inner section of Budle Bay, visible to the left — holds very large numbers of greylag geese and waders like the bar-tailed godwit.

Turn right and walk along the high tide mark.

The beach begins stony but soon turns to fine sand with a scattering of dolerite pebbles. To the right, small dunes are formed by the growth of 'dune-fixing' plants like sea rocket (which has a distinctive flower with four white or mauve petals). Once sand has accumulated around the base of the plant the mound may be colonised by the characteristic dune grasses like sand couch and lyme grass.

Behind the dunes is a cliff of boulder clay (dumped during the last Ice Age), and there are nests of sand martins dug into the more vertical sections. They excavate the holes by flying headlong at the cliff and pecking away patiently to a depth of a yard or more.

Continue along the tideline, past some limestone exposures, towards Heather Cottages. Just before the cottages, leave the tideline and take the path to the right of a marram-covered dune mound and to the left of the cottages.

Beneath the terrace of cottages is a marshy area, colonised by great hairy willowherb and horsetail. The latter is a curious plant with a sporehead rather than a flower, and has changed little over the past few hundred million years. Fossils of carboniferous horsetails look much the same as modern ones – just a lot bigger.

The path bears to the left of a small building, then opens out into a flat, dish-shaped area where boats and old tractors are parked.

Budle Bay

Marshy depressions among sand dunes are called slacks and often contain rare plants. This one is probably too small and too well-trodden, but a close look in the spring may reveal tiny forget-me-nots or violets.

On the far side of the slack the path continues between loose sandy slopes.

Between midsummer and autumn, sand wasps are common here. They are yellow and black-banded, but are very much thinner than ordinary wasps and are a lot faster in flight. They are not social, which means there is no queen or worker; each female makes her own burrow and provisions this with flies. Every burrow contains 7 or 8 cells, each with its own wasp egg and a supply of flies to last through the larval stage. The prey is paralysed rather than killed to ensure that the grub always has a supply of fresh meat. Often, 'stunned' flies can be seen lying around on the loose sand; these will have been dumped because they are too big or because the wasps dropped them on their final approach to an entrance burrow.

Back onto the tideline, the old quay is just ahead to the north. Walk onto it for a fine view of the outer bay.

Budle Bay, looking towards the Kyloe Hills

The old quay was once important as a loading point for grain and whinstone (from Kittling Hill quarry). Foundations of granaries and crushing machinery can be found in the immediate area but little is known of their history.

Continue north-east along the high water mark as far as Black Rock.

This is a large slab of dolerite – part of the Whin Sill that forms Kittling Hill and Bamburgh, a little further round the headland. It is a marvellous place to sit and gaze out to sea, the great sweep of Ross Back Sands leading the eye away to Holy Island and Lindisfarne Castle.

In the foreground is Budle Water, and just across from this is a spit of sand that seems to be a favourite roosting place for eider duck and terns. During the autumn, arctic skuas take up residence in the area. These are big dark brown birds, too sharp-winged to be gulls and much more agile in flight. They are pirates and obtain their food by chasing terns and making them drop their own hard-earned sand eels. Terns are very agile themselves, and the chase often involves incredibly complex manoeuvres, but the skua usually wins in the end.

Retrace your steps a little way, back to the quay. Turn left, walking inland along an indistinct sandy track until you reach a small caravan park. Turn left.

The concrete structure on the left was part of the quarry machinery. Just after it is a gorse covered mound with a wall of whinstone boulders. This has been colonised by storksbill and vipers bugloss – two plants that thrive in sandy places.

Carry on along the path until you reach a gun emplacement (1940s vintage). Go to the right of it and immediately sharp right up onto the edge of the golf course. Go round to the right of the greens, then right to a gateway. This leads onto a metalled road with caravans to the right. Bear left along the road.

The farm to the left is Newtown Farm, surrounded by hay meadows. The main hay crop is cut just as the grass is flowering and when the leaves still have some juice in them, usually in late June.

The road leads down to a gate, with caravans and Heather Cottages to the right. Turn left, and continue up towards a gate. Go through this and onto the main road, at which turn right.

The trees on the roadside are a curious assortment. Most are Swedish whitebeam, which has orange berries in the autumn and is noted for its ability to tolerate polluted air; it does well in such places as Eldon Square in the middle of Newcastle. Why it has been planted here is a mystery.

The other common roadside tree here is the Wheatley elm, which is another alien but has attractive dwarf leaves, like a bonsai variety of common elm.

Continue along the right-hand side of the road verge (with Budle on the left) until you arrive back at the starting point.

Sand-wasp

6 Holy Island: Lindisfarne Priory-Emanuel Head; return along the Straight Lonnen

4 miles, about 3 hours. A circuit around the eastern end of the island, best appreciated on clear winter days but just as attractive in the spring and early summer. It is an advantage to be interested in early Christian history or wildlife, but the subtle romance of the place usually seduces everyone in the end. Make sure your arrival and departure coincide with tide crossing times; under ideal conditions it is much more interesting and exciting to be on the island when the tide is in.

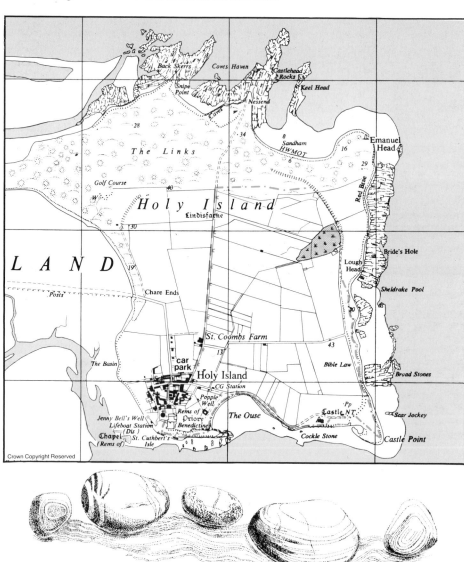

Lindisfarne Priory

Park at the island's main car park, signposted from the main road. From the car park turn right, then left onto the main road again. At the end of the main road turn right, then take an immediate left turn, down to the market place.

The township has had a very chequered history. Apart from its eminence in Anglo-Saxon times its most prosperous period came in the 19th century, when it seems to have acquired a reputation similar to that of the frontier towns of the Wild West. No policeman or doctor would stay for very long; there were frequent fights between fishermen and quarrymen, possibly as a direct result of there being at least 10 inns.

The Market Cross, with its impressive fence, was erected in 1828 as a replacement for a much more ancient stone. The socket is original, however, dating from the middle of the 16th century.

Beyond the cross, follow the notice to Lindisfarne Priory.

The priory ruins can be appreciated quite adequately from St. Mary's Church, to the right (west), but enthusiasts of Christian history will probably want to walk in the footsteps of St. Aidan who arrived here from Iona in 635. The present structure would not have been here in the early 7th century, of course – Aidan and his contemporaries built in wood and their first church must have been a very modest affair. Whilst Aidan was away converting Celts, (he once baptised 15,000 in a week), his monks stayed on the island developing a tradition for outstanding art and learning, and their influence went far beyond Northumbria. For a while the whole of Europe looked towards this tiny centre of civilisation, and its effect was incalculable.

The Vikings finally put an end to the priory in 875; the monks saw distant fires and had just enough time to collect together their precious relics (mostly saints' bones) and make for the mainland before the enemy arrived. The monks never came back, and it was not until 1093 that the great stone priory and church were built.

Walk round to the west side of the church (the tower side) and make for a gateway in the stone wall on the right.

The graves in the churchyard are a fascinating reminder of how close the links once were between the island and the sea. Apart from fishing, the less respectable business of 'wrecking', – plundering whatever ships came aground – was a traditional pastime, but the sea had a habit of claiming back many of the protagonists and the inscriptions on the gravestones often understate tragic events.

Go through the gateway, turn left, and continue down the winding track to a grassy shelf.

St. Cuthbert's Island (once called Hobthrush) stands just a little way out to sea to the south-west, though it is joined to the main island at low tide. Cuthbert was appointed Prior in 673 and was the sixth Bishop of Lindisfarne. He is probably the most famous saint in the north-east, yet he spent very little of his time in the monastery and was much happier living the life of a hermit. He spent whole days in prayer on this little islet, but eventually even this was not sufficiently remote and he took himself off to Inner Farne. According to Aelfric, Cuthbert 'was wont that he would go in the night to the sea, and stand in the salt flood to his neck, chanting his prayers'. This was considered pious rather than foolhardy.

If the tide is in, eider ducks will be all around the islet, loafing or dozing on the shore-line. They were a favourite of Cuthbert's, and are still known locally as 'Cuddy's ducks'.

Eider Duck.

Turn left up a stony path to the top of 'The Heugh'.

The rock is dolerite, similar to the Whin Sill but this time pushed up vertically as volcanic lava to form a steep-sided dyke, slow to erode. The plants growing in the nooks and crannies reflect both the kind of rock (basic rather than acidic) and the closeness of the sea: lots of thrift, sea campion and polypod fern, but also a thick sprinkling of wallflower – presumably introduced by someone to add an extra splash of colour, or a garden escapee which did well.

Along the top of The Heugh, go to the right of the coastguard building, past a storm beacon, and down again, coming out alongside a large black-tarred fishery shed.

The air is distinctly crab-flavoured around here. The stony road ahead is lined with upturned boats with doors set into them, like a set for a scene from *David Copperfield,* and there are lobster and crab pots everywhere. The inner harbour (called The Ouse) was once a much busier place and its heyday was in the 1860s. At that time, according to Richard Perry, 'a man could walk on upturned herring barrels for half a mile from the great red bricked curing house on the green above the Ouse to the Castle jetty'. It was an evil-smelling, garbage-infested place and there was little money in it for the fishermen. Little wonder that the industry declined earlier here than on the mainland coast.

Walk along the grassy track bearing right around the Ouse, and meet the road as it makes its way eastward from the village. Bear right, towards the castle.

To the south, across the flats, is Ross Back Sands. The needles were built as navigation aids, so that the fishing boats could align themselves for a safe entry into the harbour.

Go through the gate at the road end and up towards the castle.

Beblowe Hill is another section of the dolerite dyke, rising to 100 feet (30m) above sea level.

It is dominated now by a surprisingly small castle, built around 1539 to guard the harbour and lacking any pedigree of bloodshed. The garrison of the castle was never more than a handful and it must have been an uneventful posting, apart from occasional epidemics ('sudrie sogers buryed' says the church record one day in 1639, as if it were a regular event).

The nearest the castle came to battle was in October 1715, when Launcelot Errington and his nephew found all but two of the garrison out for the day and succeeded in ejecting them. For 24 hours they held the castle for the Jacobites, then made an unsuccessful run for it before the troops arrived.

Beblowe Hill and Castle, Holy Island

During the middle of the 17th century, Captain Rugg was the governor. He was, to quote just one account 'a notable good fellow, as his great read nose ful of pimples did give testimony'.

Take the path to the right of the castle; this provides a good view to the south.

The Farne Islands stand out clearly if the day is fair; a group of 15 individual islands at high tide, inhabited by seabirds and seals, and, during the summer, boatloads of humans. The Longstone Light, red with white stripes, should be visible to the left, whilst the white lighthouse of Inner Farne marks their most southerly point.

The dolerite cliffs of Beblowe Hill are colonised by fulmars, and from the path it is possible to look down onto them as they sit on their ledges. The island dwellers of St. Kilda killed large numbers and salted them away for winter food. They also used the fat and oil for fuel and lighting, which shows how appallingly hard their life-style must have been. Young fulmars defend themselves by squirting evil-smelling oil through their nostrils, and it must have taken a high degree of desperation to regard them as an attractive alternative to starvation.

Bear right of the next outcrop of dolerite and walk over the grassy area to the fenced square of lime kilns (they can be viewed from below as directed on the notice board).

This impressive battery of kilns was built by a Dundee firm in the 1850s. The limestone came by tramway from a quarry on the north side of the island, whilst the coal came from Dundee as a return cargo for the lime. This large-scale industry augmented or replaced existing operations that had made use of local island coal.

Bear right to Castle Point, the flat expanse at the south-east tip of the island.

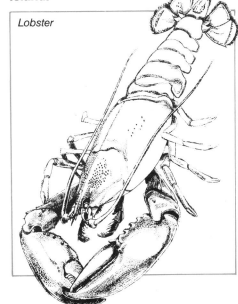
Lobster

The storm beach contains all sorts of rocks and boulders. Many contain fossils – especially crinoids, known locally as St. Cuthbert's beads because they resemble the beads of a rosary broken as he was walking on the beach. During the winter, this is a good place to watch sea-duck – eider, scoter and long-tailed duck – as they dive for shellfish in the sheltered waters between the Farne Islands and Lindisfarne. The male and female long-tailed duck were once known locally as Jackie and Jenny Foster.

Follow the coast to the left (north). Walk on the grassy ridge above the shallow clay cliff for about 250 yards (228m), then cut across to the left and follow the path below a fence-line.

This leads past Holy Island Lough, a shallow freshwater lake. In the spring it is edged with great floating carpets of mares-tail and bog-bean, and is colonised by black-headed gulls. During the winter a herd of whooper swans (from Iceland) usually takes up residence.

Just past the marshy area is a stile. Go over this and bear left along the old wagonway for about 200 yards (182m), then go through a wicket gate and after a further 100 yards (91m) look for a wide grassy path crossing the wagonway, turn left and take the path which bears right.

The white pyramid to the right is the beacon on Emanuel Head, visible for many miles around. The dunes are inhabited by a very large colony of rabbits. They were once a very valuable resource, so much so that in 1635 Brereton's

Journal describes the island as 'not worth more than 100£ a year, besides the warren, which is 40£ per annum.'

During the early summer, caterpillars of the garden tiger moth, known as woolly bears or (in Old English) wol bodes, are very common among the dune plants. The adult moths are very colourful (cream and brown with red under-wings), but are rarely seen because they are nocturnal. Cinnabar and burnet moths are both day flying species, however, and are common here in June and July. Both are deep green with red markings.

Keep the edge of the dunes to the right. This leads to a junction with a wide lane, called the Straight Lonnen.

If there is time, the area to the right, towards the north shore of the island, is worth exploring. There are cliffs, caves and old quarries, wide sandy bays backed by mature dunes and, further west, the narrow neck called Shell Road that joins the main island to the Snook.

Turn left along the Straight Lonnen at the National Nature Reserve notice board.

The centre of the island is a network of fields bounded by stone walls and old hawthorn hedges. Birds of prey, like merlin and sparrow-hawk, often hunt along the lines of the walls, pouncing on small birds that have not managed to find a safe roost.

Continue south, past the junction with the Crooked Lonnen and back to the car park.

Cheviot Hills, from Cockenheugh near Holburn

The Inland Walks

The coast becomes addictive after a while, but there are some fine walks inland, often with very dramatic views to the east and west. Beyond the 'corn belt' rises a chain of hills, running parallel to the coast and composed predominantly of Fell Sandstone. Walks 7-9 are circular routes over these areas of moorland, providing outstanding views of the Cheviot Hills and the Heritage Coast. In the north, the walk from Holburn Grange looks out over the Kyloe Hills but is dominated by woodland and rough heath. Further south, two walks have been included over Bewick Moor, perhaps the most romantic and windswept tract of heather moorland in the county and of great wildlife and historical interest. Walk 8 is comparatively straight-forward, based on a route to and from Blawearie, whilst Walk 9 requires greater fortitude but, once completed, will abide in the memory as a notable achievement – or an endurance, depending on the weather.

Remember that the grouse-shooting season starts on August 12th; please be careful if you are out on the moors when a shoot is on.

7 Holburn Grange - Swinhoe Farm ; return via Fawcet Hill

5½ miles, about 4 hours. A very varied walk through forest, pasture and open moorland with outstanding views of the Cheviot Hills and a wide stretch of the coast. An easy walk considering its length, along wide trackways with few hills to climb.

Green track from Holburn Grange

Park at Holburn Grange – a small National Trust car park (GR 051352) is sited just after the row of cottages, through a gate to the left. Out from the car park, turn left through the gate and up a wide over-grown lane towards Greensheen Hill.

This lane was probably a drove road to Belford and is typical of many moorland approaches which now seem disproportionately wide and come to an abrupt end on an open hillside. The hedge is in remarkably good shape, originally planted with hawthorn but now including a few elders and elms that have grown from wild seedlings. As a general rule, each new species of tree in a 30m stretch of hedge adds 100 years to its age, so this one is perhaps over 200 years old and is still in its prime. The flower-rich verges, full of tall herbs like meadow cranesbill and hogweed, attract butterflies and birds.

At the end of the lane, go through the gate and turn right, following the path signposted 'St. Cuthbert's Cave'.

The view back towards Holburn, with the dome of Doddington Moor in the foreground, takes in the whole of the Cheviot range, from the Scottish border down to Simonside.

In the middle and late summer the path traces its way through tall bracken, and on warm sultry days great clouds of flies seem to be on the lookout for walkers. They are not biting flies but are still the subject of a great deal of futile swatting.

Follow the path through a gate and into a mature pine plantation, marked on the left by a National Trust sign. Half way through the wood take the path to the left which leads up to St. Cuthbert's cave.

In the 7th century Cuthbert was in the habit of getting away from it all, leaving Lindisfarne to the other monks and seeking solitude in this damp, shallow cave. The roof of the cavity is held in place by a pillar of weathered sandstone.

The graffitti suggests that the cave reached its greatest popularity in the middle of the 19th

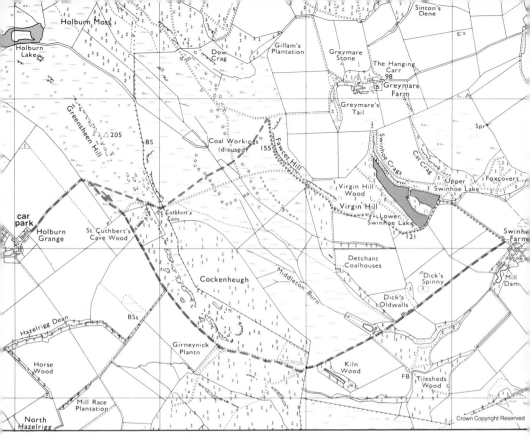

century, when railway travel brought a whole new wave of Victorian vandals out from the cities.

Retrace your route down the hillside. Back on the main path, turn left to the end of the plantation, then continue along the grassy track between a forest plantation to the left and arable farmland to the right.

The trees to the left are mostly larch – the only coniferous tree to lose its leaves in the winter. A wide clearing in this hillside plantation reveals a fine assortment of sandstone crags and blocks, heavily sculptured by wind and frost. This is the south-west side of Cockenheugh, a typical outcrop of Fell Sandstone, always facing its steep scarp slope towards the Cheviot and stretching in a wide arc down to Simonside. It was laid down as sediment in the shallow estuary that surrounded the massive volcanic dome of Cheviot. Most of the Kyloe Hills, 3 or 4 miles north of here, are of dolerite and were

Moorhen

37

St. Cuthberts cave

pushed up ('intruded') into the layers of the sedimentary rocks, but Cockenheugh is higher than any of the dolerite hills and is entirely sandstone.

Carry on along the track, which bears left to take the easiest line between Cockenheugh and Dancing Green Hill.

The trees on either side obscure any view and the woodland is dull, but the rabbit-cropped turf contains attractive flowers like heath speedwell and eyebright. The latter was once used as a remedy for blood-shot eyes because the flower, being purple with 'yellow spots and stripes' was supposed to resemble a diseased eye. According to Gerard's Herbal of 1597, eyebright 'preserveth the sight, increaseth it, and being feeble and lost it restoreth the same', but like most magic of the time it probably did more harm than good and caused more spots and stripes than it cured.

Continue to the end of the forested area, bearing left to a gate with rough grass-land and scrub to the left and arable farmland to the right. Go through the gate and make your way along the track, with the stone wall to your right.

The small pine plantation to the right is Kiln Wood. Modern forest planting has covered many archaeological sites; this area was once part of a thriving mining community with such seams as the Fawcett, Black Hill and Cooper Eye. They were thin seams and heavily faulted, but they provided vital coal to fuel the lime kilns and keep the nearby villagers warm.

The track crosses arable farmland and makes its way towards yet another pine plantation. Go through the gate and up the well-worn forest road between pine and spruce trees, over the Middleton Burn and up towards Dick's Oldwalls.

Whoever Dick was he is commemorated in both these barns (which were almost certainly built on very old foundations) and the spinney to the left as you walk down towards Swinhoe Farm. The sea shows itself for the first time, 3 miles to the north-east.

Continue down to Swinhoe Farm, then turn sharp left.

This takes you along a wide track with a tall elm hedge to the left. On the right is an attractive wooden barn — such features are rare in

Northumberland now, but centuries ago many houses were built entirely of wood. This occasionally caused unforeseen problems. When Edward III camped here (on his way to lay siege to Berwick in 1333), there was a shortage of timber and he had at least two houses dismantled for firewood.

Ahead is a mixed plantation, mostly spruce and larch but also sycamore, ash and lime. Only the ash is a native British tree; most of the others were introduced, either for decoration or for timber. Curiously, the common lime is a hybrid between two rare native trees, the small and large-leaved limes and was developed as an ornamental tree more than 300 years ago.

The track bears left, where it leads alongside Upper and Lower Swinhoe Lakes to the right.

A screen of elm and cyprus trees obscures most of the water, but the smaller Upper Lake appears through gaps in the foliage and is particularly attractive, wooded on all sides and alive ·with the squawks of coot and moorhen. Mute swans are usually on the lake too, and are a lot more noisy than their name suggests.

An assortment of willows lines the track as it carries on by the Lower Lake. Marshy ground is often colonised by these trees, which have had a bad reputation since pagan times. The reason is obscure, but is probably something to do with their habit of whispering behind your back when you have walked past them. Not only that, but old willows are able to uproot themselves and move from one place to another:

Ellum to grieve,
Oak he do hate,
Willow do walk
If yew travels late.

Continue along the stony track, with Virgin Hill to the right, and through a gate which opens out onto moorland.

The contrast is quite dramatic after having walked through wooded country for so long. Rough acid grassland is the best description for this open area, and sheep are the only notable crop. A sandstone cliff, below Fawcet Hill, runs parallel to the path and hides any view to the north or east. Before the path reaches the next gate, however, the crag disappears and the Northumberland coast comes into view – a great sweep of sands stretching from Holy Island to Budle Bay. In good visibility, the Farne Islands can be seen to the right, beyond Bamburgh Castle, and there are usually ships on the skyline to add perspective to the scene. In poor visibility there is still plenty of interest in the view closer to the moor.

Detchant Wood is the block of conifers to the north, whilst the Kettle Burn is traced in trees beyond Greymare Farm. On the night of 23 May 1639, Charles I camped his army close by Detchant Wood on his way to Berwick.

Sandstone blocks on the south side of Cockenheugh

Track back to Holburn Grange

Before the next gate, turn three-quarters left; not along the line of the fence but sharp left to take you over the brow of the open moor. Make for the right-hand side of the fenced square through a metal gate in a wire fence, then down to the gate at the bottom of the hill.

The fescue and 'bent' grasses hide a patchwork of old mine shafts in this area. The wooded hillside ahead is Cockenheugh again. The fine white sand of Cockenheugh was once mixed with grease and sold to mowers for sharpening scythes and sickles.

Once through the bottom gate and over the drainage channel (part of the Middleton Burn that has been extended to drain Holburn Moss to the north-west), the path follows a straight fence line, aimed at the gap between Cockenheugh (left) and Greensheen (right). Make for the gate on the skyline, with the cairn on Greensheen Hill to the right.

Once through the gate the Cheviot Hills again provide the dominant landscape feature, but they will probably be in a haze now, especially if the day began still and sunny.

Bear right to avoid the corner of the pine plantation; the path takes a rather vague line through the bracken, but Holburn Grange is clearly visible and the lane gate can be reached by retracing the route from St. Cuthbert's Cave. Once through the gate, continue down to the car park.

8 Old Bewick - Blawearie; return via Harehope Burn and the south side of Bewick Hill

4 miles, about 2½ hours. An outstanding walk up to the remote and eerie ruins of Blawearie. From there, south-east close to Harehope Burn and back beneath the south-facing slope of Bewick Hill.

Park carefully at Old Bewick to avoid obstructing exits, preferably on the verge next to the farm buildings. From there walk north-east along the stony side-road with terraced cottages to the left. This ends at a gate leading up to the moor.

The name Bewick is probably derived from the Old English Beo-wic, meaning bee farm. It is tempting to suppose that heather honey was an important local industry, but the indications are that most of the moor was once forested and heather must have been much less extensive. The first Lord of Bewick rejoiced in the name of Arkle Moreal. He was granted the Lordship in 1093 after slaying Malcolm, King of Scotland. His gratitude to his king was short-lived, however, for he took part in an insurrection during 1095, after which his lands were quickly confiscated.

Go through the gate and up the trackway.

To the left is a very old wall with a line of sparse but ancient hawthorns, whilst on the opposite side is a steep tree-lined bank hiding a dried-out reservoir.

Continue along the track, through a gate, with Bewick Hill to the right.

The bracken-covered hillside rises quite steeply to a fine group of pines around Hanging Crag. Above this, on the hill crest, is the Romano-British fort of Bewick Hill. It is one of the best-preserved in the whole county, with 4 encircling ridges on its north side and a perilously steep scarp slope to the south.

Down in the valley of the Kirk Burn, a little to the north-west, is the church of the Holy Trinity – its grey roof visible among a cordon of tall trees. It was built in the 11th or early 12th century but was partly demolished by Republicans during the English Civil War, then, following some restoration, by a severe gale. The present structure, built onto the Norman ruins, dates from 1867.

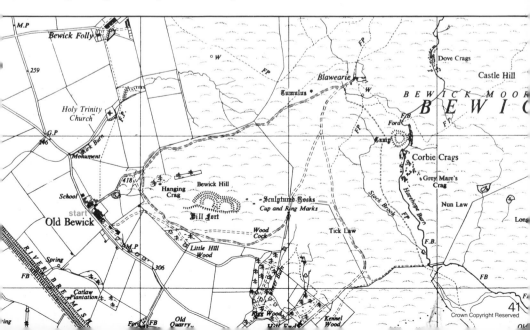

Curlew.

Blawearie, on Bewick Moor

Beyond the church and alongside the black-topped buildings is Bewick Bridge, where the River Breamish suddenly and for no apparent reason changes its name to the Till. It flows north past Chillingham, then west and north-west to meet the Tweed a few miles below Coldstream.

Go through another gate, keeping the drystone wall to your left.

The view to the north is dominated by Hepburn Wood, a Forestry Commission plantation of larch and spruce. Looking back, the Cheviot Hills are layed out like a panoramic post-card, but their confusing arrangement makes it difficult to name any individual peaks. Cheviot is the higest at 815m (2674 feet), followed by Hedgehope at 714m (2343 feet) and Comb Fell (hidden by Hedgehope) at 650m (2132 feet).

The enclosed land ends at a wicket gate alongside a replaced gateway. Go through this, keeping to the double-rutted trackway ahead.

The waterlogged ground is covered by spiky tufts of rushes – not very good food for the blackface sheep which are, however, bred to cope with austere conditions. Young heather shoots will provide them with much more palatable fare in the spring. These moors are full of grouse which also thrive on green heather.

The burning of moorland is a traditional form of management designed to get rid of tough old heather stems and to stimulate new growth. But grouse also need areas of tall heather close by in which they can nest, so a system of burning by rotation, a small block at a time, is usually employed.

Continue along the track, through heather moorland towards Blawearie.

On the ridge to the left is a small tumulus, probably Bronze Age, covered in heather but still very finely formed, bearing a burial chamber (or 'cist') at its centre. The track descends to marshy ground, across the line of a small burn, then rises to Blawearie.

42

Whoever named the steading must have been accustomed to lonely winds blowing for days on end over these high moors. Both house and byre have been derelict for 40 years; they were damaged during army exercises in the early 1940s but prior to that had already acquired a reputation for isolation. How could anyone live so far from civilisation amid a moor so full of mysterious relics? By all accounts it was not an easy life and there can have been little time for idle fancy. The last inhabitants kept a cow for milk, but the only grazing was a mile away, necessitating a 2 mile walk twice a day. No wonder they left.

The most surprising thing about Blawearie is that someone went to a great deal of trouble to construct a garden in the outcrop of Fell Sandstone close by the cottage. There are some full-sized trees, the only ones on the whole of the moor, grown to maturity now but planted with much care. There are also steps cut into the rock, providing access to a long-neglected shrubbery. Blawearie will be a place to ponder long after the roof and walls have fallen.

Lichens on a post

From Blawearie retrace your steps about 50 yards (46m) then turn left (south) over the little burn, bearing left around the lower slope of a small hill to make for the cairn on the hill, close to the remains of a Romano-British camp.

In 1865 a necklace with jet and shale beads was found nearby, together with a flint knife. This area of moorland was once quite heavily populated and there must be many more treasures awaiting discovery. On the other side of Harehope Burn is Castle Hill, the highest point on these moors.

Continue along the grassy path, with bracken either side and a radio mast on the skyline ahead. Bear right, onto the ridge between Harehope Burn and Stock Brook. This descends to an alder grove on the banks of the Harehope.

On the far side of the burn is Grey Mare's Crag; looking upstream you can see the deep gorge of Corbie Crags, providing nest-sites for kestrels and crows among cracks and fissures on the rock face.
Small birds are often uncommon on moorland; the meadow pipit is the only species that seems to thrive on the open slopes. The alder trees offer an additional habitat, however, and during the summer they are inhabited by redstarts.

Keep to the right of the burn, making for a gate in the fenceline. Turn right just before the gate and walk uphill, keeping between Tick Law and Harehope Hill, with the fence to your left. The indistinct track goes between two old hawthorn trees visible on the skyline.

Rhododendrons

Harehope Hill, to the left, was 'improved' early in the 19th century; prior to that it had been wild moorland. According to Hodgson the removal of stones and boulders uncovered several cists with some silver-hilted swords, the latter so substantially plated that the silver was stripped off and 'made into crooked sixpences by the boys of the neighbourhood'. Alas, vandalism is no new phenomenon – nor are resourceful country boys.

The track is intersected by another fenceline from the right. Turn right before the gate and walk alongside the fence to the next gate (uphill about 50 yards away). At this gate turn right along a deeply rutted bridleway: this bears to the left then gains height to Tick Law. Keep to this bridleway with the fence still visible to the left, until the fence bears off left, at which point follow the fence line until it meets a wicket gate through a drystone wall.

The view on this short section of the walk is one of the finest in the county, Blawearie to the north, open heather moors to the north-east and the Cheviot Hills away to the west. The hill directly ahead is Bewick Hill, the site of an impressive hill fort and several sculptured rocks; there are many theories relating to the origin of cup-and-ring marks on these rocks, ranging from their use as Stone Age way-marking signs to a sort of intergalactic ludo for itinerant spacemen.

Corbie Crags, Harehope Burn on Bewick Moor

Go through the wicket gate, bear half-left, and go down the hill side, then bear right along the lower slope beneath an area of rhododendron scrub.

Rhododendrons are a nuisance. They were introduced from the Himalayas by Victorians who thought they could create a much more interesting landscape than nature had provided. Inevitably the rhododendrons outlived the botanic megalomania and in many places they have shown signs of covering the hillsides. They may be pretty for a few weeks of spring but they are of little use either to stock or to wildlife.

Follow the path along the hillside, to the right of a small plantation. Keep to the same contour, not down to the fence line but about half way up the slope. Make for the lower edge of the pine trees beneath Hanging Crag; this leads to a fence. Go over the stile and turn left, back to Old Bewick.

Bewick Moor, east from Blawearie

9 Bewick Moor: Quarryhouse to Harehope; return via Cateran Hill

7½ miles, about 5 hours. Wild and remote moorland, totally unspoilt, with views of the coast, Cheviot and Simonside Hills. Boots are advisable; choose your day carefully to avoid misty weather, take a compass, and be prepared for an exhilarating but difficult walk.

Park on the wide verge on the north side of the Chillingham/North Charlton road, just west of Quarryhouse Farm, where a wide green track angles south over the moor. Walk along the track, an old drove road, heading south-west.

There are several dish-shaped depressions, mainly to the left of the track. These are the remains of small 'bell-pits', dug out to extract coal during the 17th or 18th centuries.

Away to the right (west) are the Cheviot Hills, the neat dome of Hedgehope on the left and the higher but less elegant whale-back of Cheviot on the right. Ahead, hidden amid a cluster of trees, stands Blawearie – a deserted steading and the objective for the first part of the walk.

Like many moorland tracks, this one seems to lead straight into a bog, having first picked its way between small rocky

outcrops. **In fact, the track carefully avoids the wet ground, circling round to the left.**

Rich green patches of ground are always the most dangerous: the bright colour means there must be a lot of water just beneath the layer of *Sphagnum* moss. *Sphagnum* is the most characteristic of all the bog plants, forming tussocks or complete carpets and holding water like a sponge. Cranberry, sundew, cottongrass and asphodel all grow in these wet places, but heather prefers somewhat drier ground.

The track leads down into a shallow basin with open moorland on all sides, but the trees of Blawearie should still be visible to the south-west.

The ground is much drier here, hair moss and lichen among the heather instead of

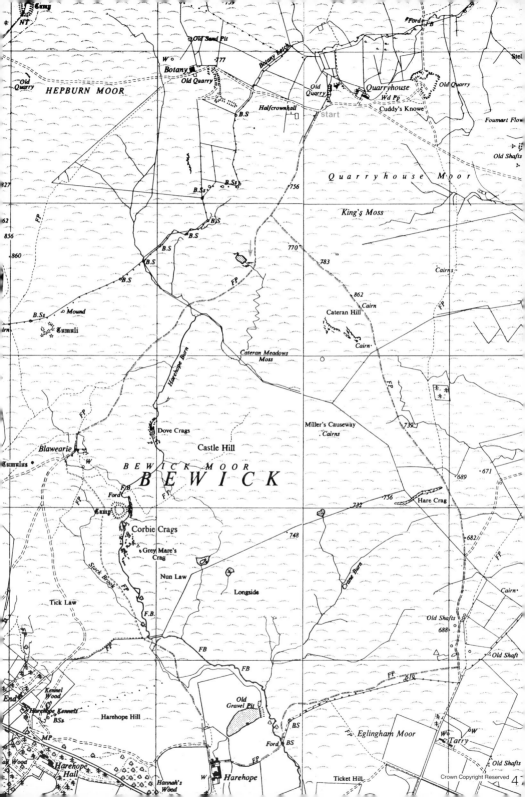

4

Sphagnum, and the peat looking more like potting compost than Guiness-coloured porridge. Hepburn Moor is away to the right and Bewick Moor to the left — the boundary is completely artificial, of course.

Continue along the track, over a small burn and through a gate (through the only fence on this part of the moor). Make for a distinct notch in the skyline, passing a large boulder on the left.

The ground begins to rise again and the track, no longer as distinct as it was, leads through a broad patchwork of heather — some recently burnt off, some mature. Red grouse thrive here but are only likely to be seen as they fly away. Their call, a low-pitched rattle followed by a few strangled sobs, is supposed to sound like 'go back, go back, go back'.

Where the ground is sandy and dry there are colonies of tiger beetles, hyper-active green creatures which buzz low over the heather and don't act like ordinary beetles at all. They are predatory, feeding on other insects, so they are fast and agile with formidable mandibles.

Over the ridge at a new trackway, turn left to Blawearie.

The natural outcrop of Fell Sandstone provides the only sheltered site for miles; Blawearie was built here as a shepherd's house and small-holding, with a byre and paddock to make it as self-sufficient as possible. No-one has lived here for 40 years and it has developed an atmosphere of desolate isolation. A garden was cut into the rocks to the east of the steading, and it is possible to sit on the outer sandstone block

and look out over Harehope Burn and Castle Hill, a view that has changed little over the past 300 years.

This area was once the property of Tynemouth Priory. It was heavily wooded, at least in part, providing 'husbote and heybote' (timber for building repairs and fencing). This was in the 13th century, but after the Dissolution of the Monasteries it was still producing good crops of timber. In 1592 it was leased by the Crown to Ralph Grey, but the Crown obviously considered the forest extensive enough to reserve 'all big trees, underwood and sapling oaks fit to be timber and sufficient "studdell" in every acre of woodland according to the statute'. This is the last reference to any trees in the Bewick area, and the actual site of the forest has been totally lost.

Red Grouse

Bewick Moor

Harehope Burn, Bewick Moor

Retrace your steps about 50 yards (46m) then turn left (south) over the little burn, bearing left around the lower slope of a small hill to make for the cairn on the hill, close to the remains of a Romano-British camp.

Continue along the grassy path, with bracken either side and a radio mast on the skyline ahead. Bear right, onto the ridge between Harehope Burn and Stock Brook. This descends to an alder grove on the banks of the Harehope. Keep to the right of the burn, making for a gate in the fence.

There are several small bogs in the shallow valley of the burn, often covered with *Sphagnum*. The small round or heart-shaped leaves are of marsh violet. The beautiful pale mauve flowers are only out in the spring, but the dark green leaves last all summer.

The thicket of trees and bushes around the burn shows that the soil is much richer in nutrients here. Birds like the redstart nest in the old stumps and feed on insects amongst the foliage.

Go through the gate, bearing left down onto the haughland, cross the broken-down wall and make for the shallow gap at the base of Harehope Hill to the right. Cross the mill stream and, with a fence to your left, continue until Harehope Farm is in sight. The fence becomes a stone wall; keep alongside the wall and through a gate to the left. Continue towards Harehope Farm, with the wall now on your right.

The marshy ground to the north-east of the farm was once a pond, constructed in the 1770s to provide water power for threshing machines. There was a great deal of ill-feeling between the farmer, and the miller from Eglingham, who used the same water supply and must have viewed this part of the agrarian revolution with some misgivings.

Go through the gate and immediately left; there is a terrace of farm cottages on the left and another gate ahead. Go through this, into a grass field with a fence, left through another gate and continue beside the fence (to the right) which changes to a drystone wall. Turn left at the end of the field, then take the footbridge, right, over Harehope Burn. Go through a gate, rejoin the drystone wall and follow this up over rough moorland. The path is indistinct but usually runs about 15 yards (10m) parallel to the wall. Keep to the right of the small conifer plantation, continuing to gain height eastwards. The path does not make for the top of the hill but continues to the right of it to meet a farm road.

The green mound and shallow pits are the remains of mine workings. The tradition dates back at least to 1783 but the scale of operations was comparatively small, at least by modern standards.

At the road, turn left and walk along the verge for about ½ mile (0.8km) with telephone wires to the left. This leads to a gate; go through this and bear half left, leaving the road and heading towards the distant cairn on the top of Cateran Hill. Hare Crag is in the foreground – make for its right-hand side, but if the ground in front is boggy keep closer to the drystone wall on the left, then cut across in front of the crag to regain the correct line.

During the spring, male emperor moths will be on the wing, dashing at breakneck speed over the heather in a reckless search for females. Later in the summer the fat green and black-banded caterpillars, about 6cm long, will be sunbathing on heather shoots, but their camouflage is very effective and they are not easy to spot.

The long expanse of heather presents a hard walk over a very obscure path. The ground rises to a fence-line. Go through the gate, past a small cairn to the left, and up onto Cateran Hill.

The view is exceptionally good, with fine moorland all around and a view of the coast, especially of Bamburgh and the Farne Islands, if it is a clear day. Black grouse occur on this part of the moor, and it is isolated enough for there to be a good chance of seeing birds of prey like merlin and peregrine.

Continue north-west, parallel to the crags.

Somewhere to the right is Cateran Hole, a cave that is supposed to lead to the Henhole on Cheviot, and there are many strange stories (unless you believe in fairies?) about the adventures of people attempting the journey.

The whole of the northern side of Bewick Moor should be visible from this side of Cateran Hill. Head north-west, keeping to the left of Quarryhouse Moor, with the farm beyond. If your car is not immediately apparent, head slightly to the left of the tall television mast until you reach the green track, then bear right back to the starting point.

Lichen

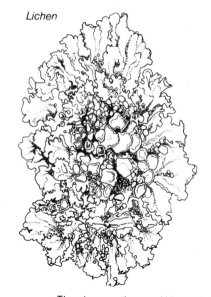

The view south over Alnmouth ▷

The Northumberland Coast Walk;
Alnmouth-Budle

Tracks tell stories: this is where a family of foxes has been playing

The Northumberland Coast Walk; Alnmouth - Budle

The long coast walk begins at Alnmouth and ends at Budle, 25 miles of constantly changing, consistently excellent landscape.

In many ways the walk follows a natural route around a broad-based promontory on the shoulder of Northumberland. Alnmouth Bay to the south and Budle Bay to the north provide natural parameters; between them the walk includes varying combinations of golden sands, secluded bays, dunes, carrs, cliffs, marshes and boulder-strewn headlands. Every two or three miles there is a village, often little more than a public house and a cluster of cottages. Accommodation is usually available, particularly at the larger places like Embleton which can therefore act as an overnight stop on a weekend walk.

More than anything else this longer route offers an opportunity to get to know the coast in its varied moods. The middle part of the day, when people are usually out walking, is the time of least activity for birds and animals. The fading light of a spring or autumn evening is a quite different matter, however; things are on the move, hunting, feeding, travelling to and fro and providing opportunities for quiet observation. Dawn or dusk is also the time to appreciate major landscape features, when oblique sunlight throws castles and kilns into relief and adds tones and colours rarely experienced inland.

An alternative to a 2-day walk involves the completion of short sections of the route on different occasions, allowing for a less strenuous but equally pleasing walk, perhaps over consecutive weekends or spaced through different seasons. Whatever strategy is adopted the long coast walk is likely to become a classic, both for its achievement and for its beauty.

FARNE ISLANDS

Staple Sound

Inner Sound

Elwick · Ross

Budle Bay

Middleton

Waren Mill

Easington

Budle

Castle

Bamburgh

253

T

Monks House Rocks

Spindlestone

Burton

Bradford

Seahouses

Carr End

Bellshill

Elford

North Sunderland

Lucker

Adderstone

A

Newham Hall

A

Beadnell

Twizell Ho

Warenford

Newham

Swinhoe

Benthall

Rosebrough

Newstead

Chathill

Fleetham

T

Beadnell Bay

394

Ellingham

Preston

High Newton by-the-Sea

Snook Point

R

Brockdam

Brunton

St Mary's or Newton Haven

Middle Moor

Doxford

Christon Bank

T

Embleton Bay

876

Cateran Hill

North Charlton

Embleton

Dunstanburgh Castle

West Ditchburn

Harehope

Eglingham

286

South Charlton

T

Rock

Dunstan

Craster

Rennington

T

10

·553

·356

Howick

Hulne Priory

Littlehoughton

Howick Haven

Titlington

R Aln

Hulne Park

1093

Longhoughton

hawdon Hall

819

Denwick

Boulmer

Bolton

Abberwick

ALNWICK

144

Boulmer Haven

roome Park

170

Lemmington Hall

Hawkhill

Lesbury

Bilton

Alnmouth

A

Castle

828

Alnmouth Bay

Edlingham

Shilbottle

High Buston

Bigges'

587

South of Seaton Point

Start from Alnmouth Common – to the north-east of the town (signposted as the main car park along the Wynd, first left as you turn into the town and fork left after 100 yards (91m)). If you have a car, park next to the old lifeboat station, beyond the golf course. There may be a small car parking charge. Walk back about 400 yards (366m) to the junction with the main road, at which turn sharp right up the steep slope.

The footpath can be rather slippery in wet weather, and in the late summer the bracken is bound to be a nuisance, but the view from the top is exceptionally good and is a worthy starting point for this coastal walk.

Bear right (north) at the top of the ridge.

The large building is a Franciscan Friary. A little further along the path is a bench, providing a comfortable stopping point for assessing the view south.
In the distance are Coquet Island and Hauxley Point, marking the northern boundary of industrial Northumberland. Further inland is Warkworth Castle, its square tower the only clear feature at this distance, but well worth a closer look on another occasion. It began as a Norman motte and bailey, but was added to

through succeeding centuries and was the setting for part of Shakespeare's *Henry IV.*
In the foreground is Alnmouth, set on a 50 foot (15m) high promontory on the north bank of the Aln and a very ancient settlement, well past its days of glory. It was an important harbour, developed by the burgesses of Alnwick during the early 16th century, but by 1594 its condition was already giving concern to the Earl of Northumberland, who wrote to one of his officers:

'Beinge credyblie enformed that my towne of Alemouth...is nowe all most utterlye depeopled and brought to waste, partlye in respecte thatt men of the countrye for theire particular ease have bought the burgages [i.e. tenures] in Alemouth which they suffer to laye waste, caryenge from theme the profyttes of the soyle in the harvests...'.

Things improved a little, but in general there was a long period of decay until the 18th century when the harbour was used extensively for the export of grain.

Continue along the crest of the ridge, heading north-east.

After several hundred metres the footpath leads

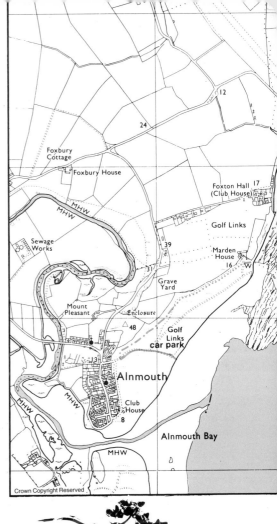

to the left of an artillery battery. From a distance this looks as if it is just another relic of the 1940s, but it was built at the beginning of the 19th century 'for the use of the Percy Artillery Volunteers'. In 1895 the battery was the venue for a gunnery competition between teams from Alnmouth and Amble. The Amble team lost but returned in the evening to smash windows in the town and police had to be sent from Alnwick to sort out the rumpus. Alnmouth acquired its own policeman for the first time following this colourful episode.

Past the battery, the path opens out onto a golf course (claiming to be the second oldest in England). Keep to the left of the green, alongside an old wall and fence, and carry on towards a derelict cottage with a small caravan park to the left.
At the cottage bear right at the gravelled track, but cut off left almost immediately along a narrow footpath through the undergrowth and down onto the beach.

The upper section of the beach here has an interesting assortment of plants, all adapted to life close to the shore. Just above the high tide mark are some miniatures that look like garden weeds: these are sand spurrey and frosted orache, capable of withstanding regular showers of salt water. Behind them, forming the first loose dunes, are clumps of lyme grass and sand couch.

Frosted Orache

57

Turn left along the foreshore.

Foxton Hall, the clubhouse of the golf course, is on the left. To the right are Marden Rocks which at low tide provide a feeding area for oyster-catchers and redshank.

Continue north, around the sandy bay with Seaton Point ahead.

Just before Seaton Point, under a field to the left, lies the body of a 53 tonne sperm whale, buried in 1973 after coming aground on the Point. It was only the thirteenth sperm whale to have been washed up on the British coast in over 100 years, but it presented local coastguards and health authorities with an unusual problem. After only a day or two the gases in its stomach had started to ferment and the indescribable smell was percolating along the coast towards Boulmer. After various disposal attempts (such as trying to blow it to pieces with explosives – which failed completely), the carcass was sectioned up and dragged to its giant grave south of Seaton House.

Looking south to Boulmer

Continue along the high tide mark around Seaton Point: there is a footpath cutting across the headland if the sea is too rough, but it is not an attractive route, past holiday huts, and is best avoided.

The south-east tip of Seaton Point is a favourite site for brittle stars – beautiful, fragile animals related to starfish, rarely noticed because they are grey in colour and live in muddy pools close to the low water mark. It is almost impossible to pick up a brittle star without it shedding 1 or more of its 5 legs. This may seem a drastic kind of defence, especially as there is little left to a starfish once its legs have gone, but they are regrown quite quickly without any permanent disability.

In December 1565 there was a shipwreck just off the Point, involving 'a great masse of golde, which was founde in one cheist, castyng upon the rocke, by the said Thomas Shippert of Howghton and the fishers of Boulmer'. It had been on its way to Mary, Queen of Scots, a figure destined for even worse fortune in subsequent years.

The best route to follow is just beneath

the low sandstone cliffs: there is a belt of sand before the rocks of Marmouth Scars begin, and this continues right around the point and into Boulmer Haven.

The red and white signs on the posts just above the beach to the left of the path are navigation aids to guide fishing boats into Boulmer Haven. Some distance to the left is the radar tracking station of R.A.F. Boulmer. It is also the base for the air-sea rescue service, and Sea King helicopters, painted bright yellow, are usually in evidence somewhere along the coast.

Follow a path alongside the fence, just above the beach, towards Boulmer.

The beach above the haven is banded by tidemarks of pebbles and shells. Many of the little pebbles are of coal, weathered from undersea seams, but there are also tiny fragments of quartz, dolerite and gritstone and, if you are very lucky, perhaps even a drop of amber – fossilised resin from the great carboniferous forests.

Most of the shells are of limpets and winkles, but on this particular beach there are also cowries. They are less than 1cm in size and are difficult to spot among other jetsam from the seabed, but they are an attractive currency for young beachcombers and make passable necklaces.

The path meets a track and bears left to a road. At the road go right, into the village.

Boulmer has a remarkably colourful history and was well known as a smugglers' rendezvous. Gin was their main import, distributed all over the country by such characters as Blind Wull Bawmer who, according to an old ballad,

     felled a' the gaugers i' Jethart
     When comin' frae Boomer wi' gin.

Boulmer (which is still pronounced Boomer) was not a safe place on a dark night.

The road leads past the Fishing Boat Inn, then turns left at a junction with a minor road. Take the minor road, which leads straight on, parallel with the coast. Continue along the track and past houses to the right, towards a gate. Go through this and northwards, keeping to the track.

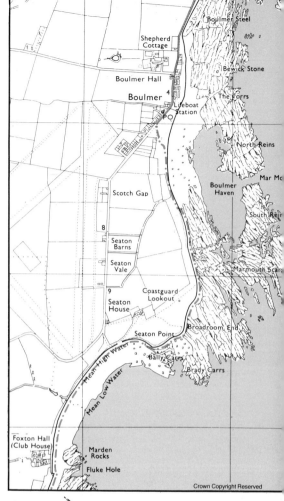

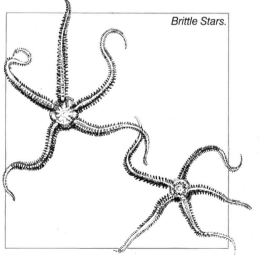

Brittle Stars.

59

Boulmer Steel, the area of rocky fissures and mud to the right, is an outstanding habitat for wading birds; they like the mud because of all the small creatures it contains. Dunlin and redshank are probably the most abundant, but there are usually turnstone, godwit and plover too. Waders have attractive calls, sounds in tune with the marshes and mudflats. The only one that can become irritating is the redshank, which produces a panic-stricken series of piping notes and is known as 'the warden of the marshes' because it is the first to fly — and call — when danger threatens. The grey plover is considered by many naturalists to have the most melodic and sad of all bird calls. Judge this for yourself; transcribed it becomes something like 'tlee-oo-ee' — not very romantic at all.

Through a gate, the track bears away from the coastline to cut off Longhoughton Steel. This time, stay with the track, keeping the wall to your left. The wall ends at a fence with a wicket gate. Go through this, over the footbridge and over the stile to the left on the other side. Follow the track north-west. This leads to a car park above Howdiemont Sands, with the road to Longhoughton leading away to the left.
From the car park cut down a path to the right, onto the beautiful beach of Howdiemont Sands.

For most of the year the only inhabitants of the beach are birds and animals: their footprints follow the tideline and provide clues about their feeding habits. The most common footprints here are of gulls, crows and waders (like the curlew and oystercatcher). Gulls have webbed feet and the back toe is very small — like ducks but with bigger claws. Crows have long back toes and long claws which drag in the sand to give a curious furrowed trail. Wading birds do not have webbed feet or an obvious back toe, and they place their feet one after the other rather than side by side to give a trail like a set of short arrowheads pointing in the wrong direction. All three dig in the sand to find food, but waders probe with their long beaks and make neat round holes, whilst gulls and crows hack away in apparent chaos.

Walk north, around the headland, keeping to the avenue of sand above the shelf of sandstone, through an area of cross-bedded sandstone and dolerite boulders to Sugar Sands.

The 'cliff' is of boulder clay (dumped during the Ice Age) and there are several freshwater springs, often stained orange from iron nodules in the underlying rock. Plants such as centaury, grass of Parnassus and butterwort flourish on the wet soil.

Onto Sugar Sands, go past the dune gap on the left then, about 100 yards (91m) past the lifebuoy, take the footpath sharp left, up to the top path. Turn right along this path, with a good view of Iron Scars (the pale grey rocks are calcareous shale) and go down to the bridge over Howick Burn.

To the left the burn winds its way down from Howick Hall. It is an attractively wooded valley, alder and sallow along the water edge and sycamore and oak higher on the banks. The rough rhubarb-like leaves on the gravels are butterbur, so called because they were used as butter wrappers before grease-proof or waxed paper were invented.

On the other side of the bridge there is a choice of routes. The coastal path has been badly eroded so either go along the boulders on the shore or continue along the track. The shoreline route is much more interesting but the boulders can make walking uncomfortable, and if the tide is high the shore may disappear altogether! Take your choice of:

ROUTE 'A' ALONG THE SHORE

The rusty relic visible on the rocks at low tide is the remains of a ship's boiler, salvaged from the wreck of the French trawler *Tadorne*. She went down on the night of 29th March, 1913; most of her crew were rescued by the Boulmer lifeboat, but 5 were drowned and are buried in Howick churchyard.

On the far side of the haven, before the sandstone cliff, turn left up a sandy path and go through the gate. Continue along the path and through another gate, with Seahouses Farm across the field to the left.

To the right is an old sandstone quarry; the stone was used to build Howick Hall and the bathing house a little way ahead. The sandstone is cross-bedded and has weathered into all sorts of strange shapes.

(See page 14 for additonal information about the next stretch of coast).

◁ *Rivulets across the sand, Howick Burn.*

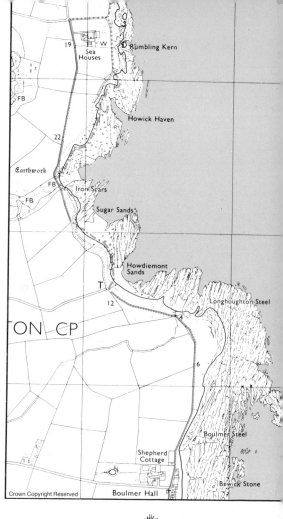

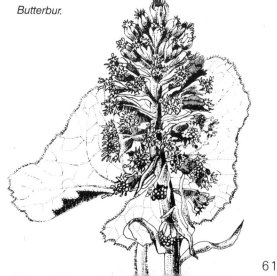

Butterbur.

61

Iron Scars, Howick Haven in distance

ROUTE 'B' ALONG THE TRACK

Go through the stone gateway, then through a gate and, with a fence to either side, continue for several hundred yards to meet a road just past Sea Houses Farm. At the road turn right, along a track signposted 'Coastal Path. Craster 2'. Through a gate at the end of the track, turn left along the coastal footpath.

The two routes converge at this point.

Continue along the well-defined coastal path, to the left of the bathing house and north-west to meet the Craster road. The track runs parallel with the road for some way, cutting through blackthorn before bearing right towards Cullernose Point.

Two types of bird nest on these cliffs. The most obvious is the fulmar, partly because it is large and gull-like (it is actually related to petrels and albatrosses), and partly because it is noisy. Each pair produce a single chick – an ugly fat creature fed on oily fish entrails until it weighs far more than its parents.

The other cliff-nesting bird is the house martin, which looks strangely out of place here. In fact this is one of the few 'natural' colonies in the whole of Britain, making use of overhanging cliffs and catching insects in flight over the grassland. If it were not for buildings and quarries, the house martin could be one of our rarest birds.

At Cullernose the path climbs onto the ridge of Long Heugh. Through a gate, turn right towards the coastguard hut. Keep left of the fence line and cut off the corner (of the Point) by turning left at the hut. This brings you back onto the coastal path, though the short-cropped turf makes it difficult to see its actual line.

Continue north through another wicket gate until just south of Craster, where the path turns abruptly left and then bears right to regain the coastline. Over a stile,

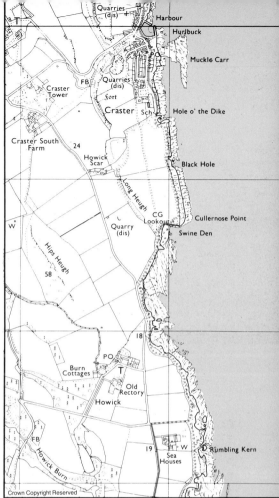

with the village school to the left, continue until you reach the football field at which point cut across left onto the road. Turn right and go on to the end of the road, then turn right and immediately left and into the centre of Craster.
In Craster, take the main road north, around the harbour.

Fishing and quarrying were the industries of Craster; both used the harbour, built between 1906 and 1912, but the whinstone (dolerite) quarries were a comparatively brief phenomenon, closing down 40 years ago. On the end of the south pier is the concrete base of what was a tall loading hopper, linked by a cableway to the quarry and dismantled at the beginning of the Second World War because it was considered a potential navigation aid to enemy aircraft. The fishing fleet at Craster is only a fraction of what it once was; kippering at Craster now relies on herring from the west of Scotland. Before the Second World War, 25 women of the village were employed between June and September, each cleaning 2,000 fish a day. This process is now done by machine but the actual kippering is much as it always was, the fish hung on tenterhooks over slow-smouldering oak sawdust.

Seaweed-covered stone

Dunstanburgh, from Oxberrylaw

The main road bears left out of Craster, but a cul-de-sac continues parallel with the coast. Take this smaller road past a row of houses on the left and to a gate. Go through this and along the coastal path heading north.

The ridge on the skyline to the left is a whinstone heugh, Oxberry Law. The gently sloping grassland this side of the heugh is its dip slope, exposed as it meets the sea in a wide shelf of very hard grey dolerite.

Continue north, through a gate, to bear right around a small sandy bay called Nova Scotia.

Dunstanburgh Castle dominates the view ahead. Its outer perimeter was a sea-filled moat, barely visible now but once an important defensive feature. There was also a small harbour, situated this side of the rocky outcrop of Castle Hill, which has been land-locked and dry for many years and must have been small even by Tudor standards.

Keep to the path as it makes its way up towards the castle.

If you have time, cut across the grass to the right-hand (eastern) edge of the castle, which provides an interesting view of Queen Margaret's Cove and Egyncleugh Tower (the name refers to the medieval name for the cove). There was a drawbridge across the moat from this tower, and the gateways on its inner and outer walls suggest it was an important entrance to the castle, probably with its own barbican. The cove was where 'Dunstanburgh diamonds' were excavated. They can still be found today – no more than quartz crystals, of mythical rather than material value. (For additional information about Dunstanburgh, see page 18).

From the keep (the main entrance to the castle) bear left, around the landward side of Castle Hill. The path continues beneath the Lilburn Tower, then bears left as it meets the coast again before Greymare Rock.

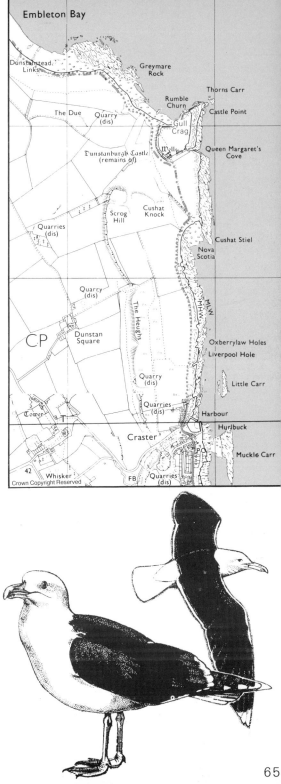

To the east is Gull Crag, a seabird colony of kittiwakes, fulmars and guillemots. Ahead, on the seaward side of the path close to the gate, is a scooped-out hollow marking the site of a machine-gun emplacement from the Second World War. Dunstanburgh was a look-out post during both wars, but it rarely saw anything of the enemy apart from an uncomfortable encounter with an aircraft which took pot-shots at soldiers laying a minefield to the west of the castle.

After the gate, the path continues northwest. Keep to the right of the golf course and follow the ridge of dunes into Embleton Bay.

The rocks at the southern tip of the bay are a favourite roosting place for gulls. The biggest is the greater black-back, distinguished by its black wings and mantle, and its pink feet. It is a scavenger and a killer, specialising during the summer in young kittiwakes and guillemots.

Great Black-back Gulls

65

Newton Point

Walk along the ridge of dunes above the bay, until the beach changes from boulders to sand, then follow one of the gaps down to the beach – taking care not to damage the marram grass or erode the dunes. Follow the high water mark until it reaches the outfall of Embleton Burn. If it is too deep to ford comfortably, walk left to the footbridge, then return to the tideline.

The large grey rock on the beach is called Bathing Rock; a little to the north-west of this is the famous 'vanishing rock' on which the name Andra Barton is carved. Barton was a Scottish pirate, killed in a sea battle with the English in 1511. King James IV was outraged, but Henry VIII seems to have been far from apologetic: 'The fate of pirates was never an object of discussion between princes' was his terse reply. Two years later the Battle of Flodden ended the dispute, when King James and 10,000 of his men lay dead following one of the bloodiest encounters in history.

The Andra Barton Rock, which has disappeared under the sand for up to 20 years at a time, was last sighted in 1974.

Continue along the tideline, bearing left around Chuck Bank with a series of rocky outcrops to the right.

Eider ducks usually roost offshore on the rocks, where they are safe from disturbance. As with most ducks, the eider has a complex mating display in which the drake throws back his head and delivers a seductive coo. This seems to have no effect whatsoever on females but triggers a lot more cooing among other males. For most of the year the male has a distinctive black and white plumage, but after the breeding season all the flight feathers are moulted, and to avoid attracting unwelcome attention from predators an 'eclipse' plumage of dull brown is adopted.

Newton Seahouses (known locally as Low Newton) will be visible to the north-west. Before this, however, just after a green hut, take the path left, cutting through the dunes. This joins a track, at which turn left past the house and walk south for about 100 yards (91m).

This brings you through an area of sallow trees

to a hide, sunk into the bank to the right and providing a view of Newton Pool: a prime vantage point for watching waterbirds and, in the spring, a large colony of black-headed gulls. The area is owned by the National Trust and there is sometimes a warden on hand to answer questions about the coastal wildlife. During the spring and summer the bushes are a favourite habitat for sedge warblers, active little birds with a distinctive eye-stripe and a chattery song. Unlike most warblers they are quite easy to see and often sit right out in the open only a metre or so from the path.

Retrace your steps northward and continue along the track into Newton Seahouses (Low Newton). If you are in a hurry take the footpath (signposted) on the north side of the road a little way north-west of the square, but this is not a very interesting walk and it is much more pleasant to follow the coast around Newton Point. To do this, go down onto the beach and head north-east over the lichen-covered limestone shelf until it is possible to walk on the turf above the rocks.

The building high on the hill to the left is a coastguard station, providing an outstanding view of the whole coast.

At Newton Point bear left, past Black Kirk Rock towards the sandy bay called Football Hole.

There is a whinstone (dolerite) outcrop on the headland. If the tide is out, look at the barnacles encrusting the rocks. They are not proper shellfish at all and are totally unrelated to limpets. They are crustaceans, relations of the crab and lobster, and spend the early part of their life floating in the sea.

Most of the barnacles are the common species called *Balanus balanoides* but in 1968 *Elminius modestus* was discovered here at Newton. This may not sound especially noteworthy, but the new species is from Australia and was only found in Britain for the first time in 1968 — probably having hitched a lift on the bottom of a boat. *Elminius* was described and named by Charles Darwin, who found time for a great deal of work on barnacles whilst he was waiting to publish *The Origin of Species*.

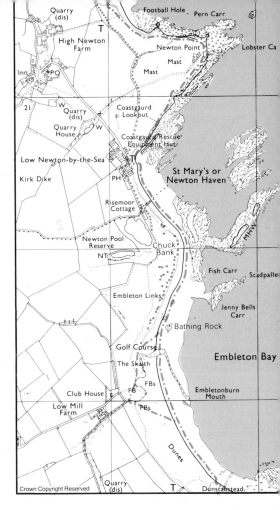

'Andra Barton' a rubbing from the inscription on the vanishing rock, Embleton Bay

6

Continue north-west, around the Football Hole, towards the Snook.

The Football Hole is one of the finest of all the small bays on the Northumberland coast, bordered by whin boulders with attractive pale golden sand. The 'scar' at the northern end is an excellent rock pool site at low tide, deep and beautiful, with a good assortment of seaweeds, fish and molluscs.

From the Snook, walk westwards through the stile and along the dune path (with a good view of Beadnell Bay to the north). This leads to another gate close to Newton Links Farm and the car park. Turn right, down to the beach.

The dunes closest to the sea suffer a great deal from windblow; further inland the marram has anchored them into place and allowed other grasses and flowers to colonise the slopes. Butterflies find these conditions to their liking, particularly the common blue which lives up to its name along this section of the coast. The female is completely different from the male,

having brown wings and a much less dashing flight; she is more interested in searching for suitable clumps of birds-foot trefoil on which to lay her eggs.

Snails are surprisingly abundant on these links. They need a good supply of calcium in order to make their shells and they get this from the pieces of seashells mixed into the sand. Where there are isolated stones, look for thrush's 'anvils' - places where song thrushes have broken open snailshells leaving a pile of fragments as evidence.

Walk north-west along the upper shore of Beadnell Bay, with Newton Links to the left. In the middle of the bay there is a wide gap through the dunes where the Long Nanny has it outfall. Do not go near to the burn: bear left, over the fence at the stile and continue along the path parallel with the burn. Take care not to go anywhere near nesting birds - this area is a Nature Reserve.

During the summer there will be nesting terns and ringed plovers among the shingle to the

Lime Kilns at Beadnell

right; a National Trust warden is usually on duty nearby.

Cross the Long Nanny footbridge and take the track north-east, inland of the dune ridge. After 500 yards (457m), at the sign reading 'Coastal Path - Long Nanny Footbridge, Newton Links House', turn right, through a wicket gate and back onto the beach.

Cowslips are quite common along the grassy verge, flowering in the spring. Coastal cowslips are much shorter than those that grow along hedgerows, presumably as a precaution against strong winds. The name cowslip is derived from 'cowslop', referring to its assumed habit of growing where cows have provided natural fertilizer. Perhaps we are lucky that some names have been cleaned - up over the years.

On the beach follow the tideline north-east towards Beadnell Point.

The wide expanse of intertidal sand seems quite lifeless, but beneath the surface there are millions of shellfish and worms. Cockles and tellins are two of the most common molluscs hiding just under the surface, but the most obvious signs of subterranean life are the small craters and casts made by lugworms. The crater marks the head shaft of a U-shaped burrow, where the worm has sucked sand down into its main 'gallery'. Once the sand has gone through its gut and any food absorbed, the worm ejects it along the tail shaft, leaving the characteristic jumble of spaghetti on the surface. Lugworms can grow up to 9 inches (about 23 cm) long and are a favourite food for fish and gulls.

Walk round to Beadnell Harbour.

Beadnell — once known as Bedinhall — developed as a fishing village, and the lime kilns which temporarily took over the place are now used to store crab pots.
In the 18th century Beadnell was an important base for smugglers: 2,700 gallons (12,274 litres) of brandy were seized by excisemen on a single night in 1762.

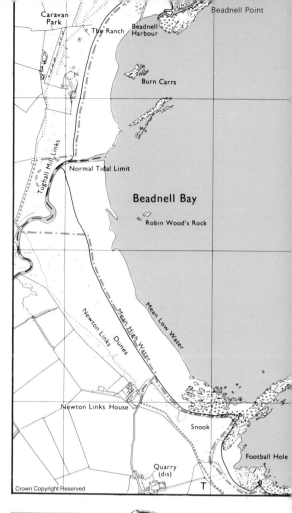

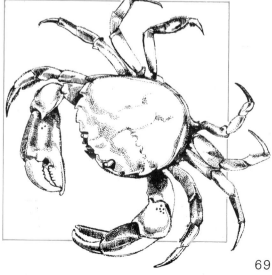

Shore Crab

Beadnell Bay

Go to the left of the kilns and walk along the grassy path to Beadnell Point – also known as Ebbe's Snook.

The small pile of grass-covered rubble near the point is the remains of Ebba's Chapel, a 13th century structure excavated in 1853 after being buried for many years. Ebba was the sister of King Oswald; she may have been responsible for the building of a small chapel on this site in the 7th century.

The stones and debris of the chapel have been colonised by thrift and scurvy-grass. As the name implies, scurvy grass was once used by sailors as a source of vitamin C, but it was also widely sold in the 16th century as a health-giving herb – despite its nasty taste. One look at the small white flowers is enough to tell it is not grass at all; in fact it is closely related to water cress.

Retrace your steps, then either walk north-west through the village of Beadnell or bear right along the boulder-strewn shore for 100 yards (91m), then join the coast road, heading north-west.

Most of the rock outcrops are of limestone, but there are several coal seams and a fine example of a dyke: a 25 foot (8m) wide wall of dolerite pushed up through the sedimentary rocks just north of Beadnell.

Continue north-west to join the B1340, the main coast road. The next section of the walk is complicated by the state of the Annstead Burn on the north side of the bay. If the tide is out the burn is only an inch or so deep, but when the tide is full it is not easy to cross and an alternative route, along the road, has to be used.

IF THE TIDE IS OUT:-

Bear right onto the sands of Annstead Bay, along the tideline.

This is one of the most heavily-used beaches in Northumberland and lacks any real character. The dunes overlie an important geological fault; the beds of limestone and shale to the north have slipped by nearly 1,000 feet (305m).

At the Annstead Burn ford the shallow outfall (not too difficult in suitable walking boots). Immediately north of the burn, at the old anti-tank blocks, turn left up onto the grassy path. The path then

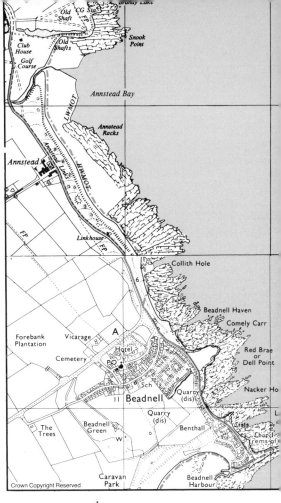

bears right, with quarry workings to the left.

IF THE TIDE IS IN:-

Continue north along the wide verge on the right side of the main road. After almost a mile (1.5km) the road crosses the Annstead Burn, and 150 yards (130m) further on, there is a path signposted to the right just before a long quarry pond. Take this footpath and follow the way-marked path past the golf clubhouse and parallel with the pond.
The path continues east, along the crest of a narrow ridge. The alternative routes converge here.

The deep pond to the left (an old limestone quarry overlying coal seams) has been colonised by emergent plants such as reeds and sedges. To the right is a solid shelf of limestone dipping sharply to the sea.
The 1844 quarrying uncovered a small cave or cell, linked by a clay conduit to a small cottage. It is reputed to have been a bolthole for Queen Margaret after Henry VI's troops had been defeated at the Battle of Hexham in 1464, but the same story is linked with several other sites in the County.

Marram Grass, Lyme Grass and Sand Couch.

71

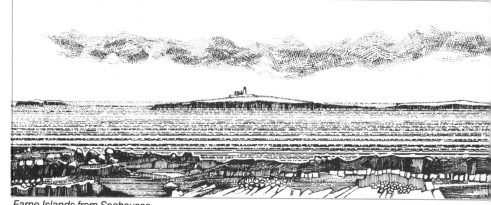
Farne Islands from Seahouses

At the end of the ridge follow the way-marked path which bears left, across the golf course. There should be no danger of stray golf balls, but be considerate to golfers teeing-off. Continue north-west, cutting off Snook Point and making for the cliff path to the right of a stone wall.

This section of the coast is surprisingly attractive, providing good views of the Farne Islands and, looking back beyond Beadnell, Dunstanburgh Castle.

At the point where the golf course ends, the cliffs are of limestone capped by boulder clay. Sand martins nest in the soft clay; they look like brown swallows with short tails and can be distinguished from young martins or swallows by their dark breast-band.

Fulmars find this part of the cliff to their liking too, sailing along on rigid wings using the updraught of wind from the sea. They often fly very close to the path, craning their necks to see what is happening, and seem to find dogs particularly interesting.

To the left is a caravan site, whilst to the right is Seahouses Point. Continue along the path, which bears left into Seahouses and leads to the harbour.

Seahouses developed as an extension of North Sunderland, the village to the south-west.

Coming into Seahouses harbour

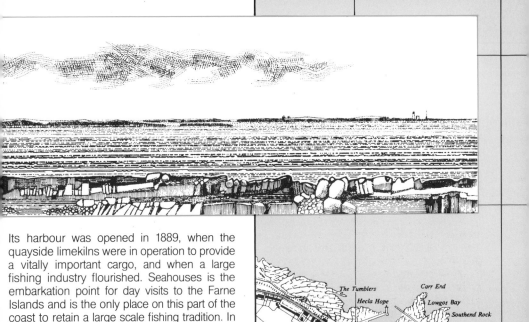

Its harbour was opened in 1889, when the quayside limekilns were in operation to provide a vitally important cargo, and when a large fishing industry flourished. Seahouses is the embarkation point for day visits to the Farne Islands and is the only place on this part of the coast to retain a large scale fishing tradition. In recent years it has become a honeypot for tourism, taking some of the pressure away from other more picturesque villages.

From the harbour bear left, up to the coast road, then turn right and head north-west on the seaward side of the road.

On the cliff path which runs alongside the road there are several seats for a comfortable view of the Farne Islands.

There are 2 major groups of islands, separated by Staple Sound, but from this position it is rather difficult to make out where one island ends and another begins. On the extreme right is the tiny islet of Crumstone, followed by the first of the 'proper' islands, Longstone, with its red and white banded lighthouse. To the left of this are the cliffs and pinnacles of Staple Island, with Brownsman (and its old lighthouse tower) behind and to the left.

Staple Sound is foreshortened from this angle. East and West Wideopen are the next significant features, followed by the high cliffs of Inner Farne with a white lighthouse and ancient tower. Megstone, standing alone to the left, is the most westerly of the rocks and completes a group of 15 true islands (another 13 appear when the tide is out).

Fulmars

73

The history of the Farne Islands is inexorably linked with the Lindisfarne monks; both St. Aidan and St. Cuthbert used Inner Farne for solitary contemplation in the 7th century, to be followed through the centuries by a succession of hermits. Today the Farne Islands are famous for their nesting seabirds and seals, and they are visited by boatloads of tourists throughout the summer. The National Trust restricts access to 2 islands – Inner Farne and Staple – in an attempt to give the wildlife a little privacy.

Approximately 300 yards past St. Aidan's Hotel, take the coastal path which bears right away from the road. When the shoreline turns from rock to sand, just before the end of the row of houses to the left, turn right down to the beach.

Oystercatchers are probably the most common birds on the rocks; they are certainly the most obvious with contrasting black and white plumage and a thick orange beak, used to split-open cockles and mussels. Many oyster-catchers nest along the river valleys of the Cheviot Hills and move down to the coast in the autumn, but others remain on the shoreline all year, their entire lives controlled by the tides.

Keep to the shoreline, heading north-west with St. Aidan's dunes to the left.

After the wide sandy beach comes a small out-crop of limestone at Shoreston Rocks. There will probably be eider ducks on the sea, feeding on the mussels attached to the rocks. On this coast mussels are washed away before they reach any size, but they still provide the staple diet for diving ducks such as eider and scaup.

Continue north-west, towards Monks House.

The 'house on the shore' stands on the site of a very ancient mill and grain store owned by the monks of Lindisfarne. It was also a ferry house and was the original embarkation point for Inner Farne, only 1½ miles to the north-east.
During the 1950s Monks House was developed

Tall dunes, near Greenhill Rocks, north of Monks House

into a bird observatory by Eric Ennion, one of our finest wildlife artists and a pioneer of Field Study Centres in Britain. Birds were caught (in a variety of nets), ringed and released, the information providing vital clues about migration. Since 1962 the complex of buildings has been split into private flats but they still retain something of their original character, a halfway house between Seahouses and Bamburgh.

Ford the very shallow Brock Burn, alongside Monks House, then head north-west along the high tide mark.

The first small outcrop of limestone has been distorted by a layer of dolerite, injected into the sediments and causing changes in their mineral structure.

During the early spring the high tide mark is often littered with the bodies of lumpsucker fish — 'singular' is a diplomatic description of their appearance; 'ugly' might be more appropriate. The males stay to guard the spawn, close to the shore, and are often stranded by the retreating tide or dashed against the rocks during storms. The dunes to the left reach their highest point here; there is an old pillbox and a coastguard station commanding a fine view of the islands — now stacked behind one another. To the right are Greenhill Rocks, covered with seaweeds such as bladder wrack, which provide feeding places for turnstones and, during the winter, purple sandpipers.

This is a good place to watch grey seals; they breed on the Farne Islands and like to 'bottle' in the water close inshore to watch people walking along the beach. Ashore, seals may seem ugly and ungainly, but in the water they are very agile — almost graceful — despite the fact that a bull grey seal may weigh over 50 stones (318kg). They are the source of a great many myths and legends, including one about a Viking saved by a mermaid from the rocks near Monks House. These days seals are viewed with hostility by some fishermen because of the damage they can do to nets.

The beach is intersected by a rolling shelf of limestone (rich in fossils). Cross this and continue along the beach, past the Islestone Rock, with tall dunes to the left. The coast turns more westerly towards Bamburgh.

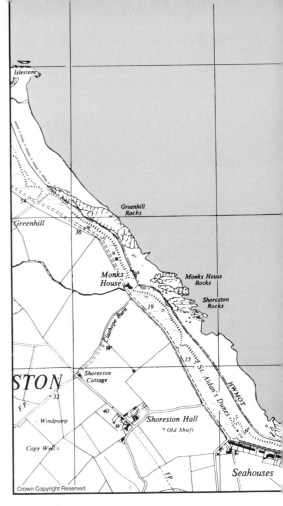

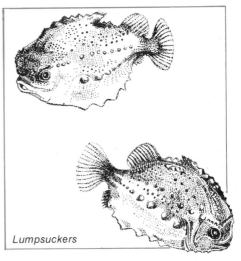

Lumpsuckers

This is the closest point to the Megstone, about 1½ miles to the north-east. It is a favourite roosting place for cormorants and shag, which dive for fish along inshore waters but like to dry their wings, standing like scarecrows, on the safety of the offshore rocks.

Just above the high tideline the beach is being colonised by clumps of sea rocket, in flower in the late summer and autumn. The seeds are dispersed by the sea and are thrown up on the drift line, where they provide food for buntings and pipits.

Higher on the beach are clumps of lyme grass and marram, and beyond the dune ridge inland stretches Redbarns Links, an area of dry sandhills and damp willowherb marsh.

Keep to the high water mark, past Bamburgh Castle.

The great angular castle sits atop a high promontory of dolerite, a strategic position guaranteeing Bamburgh a stormy history. There was an important fortification here in Anglo-Saxon times (see page 22) but nothing remains of King Ida's capital, and the oldest part of the present structure is the Norman keep. Through the Border Wars and the Wars of the Roses, Bamburgh was fought over with frightening regularity, a succession of sieges culminating in the Earl of Warwick's victory in 1464 which saw Henry VI replaced by Edward IV.

Bamburgh seems to have been the home of several powerful women who helped to shape the history of the area. In the 7th century Ethelfrith the Destroyer gave the castle to his queen, Bebba, who governed it very competently through some difficult times. In 1095 Countess Matilda held out against a siege by William Rufus and only capitulated when her husband, Robert de Mowbray, was captured and she was threatened with his being blinded. During the early 14th century a very shady period of corrupt local government saw Isobel de Vescia in control of the castle, and finally, during the 15th century, Queen Margaret avoided the Earl of Warwick on several occasions by fleeing to Bamburgh before the eventual defeat of her husband at the Battle of Hexham.

By Tudor times the castle was in a very poor state of repair, yet it was still an impressive structure. In 1550, Sir Robert Bowes recommended that it should be restored to its former status, 'for the scyte thereof is wonderfull strong and the keeping of the same castle is the best office that the kinge's matie gevethe within the east marches of England'. His advice was ignored and the castle was laid waste until restoration work in the 18th century raised it to its present picturesque state.

Patterns of sand and dolerite slab, Budle Bay

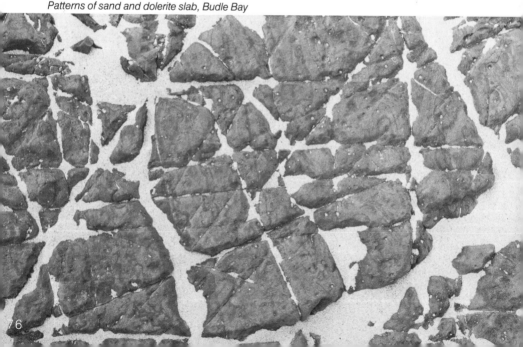

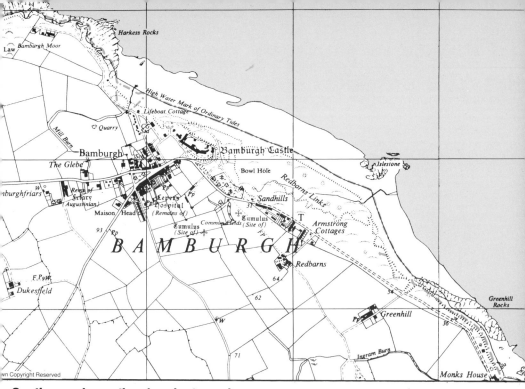

Continue along the beach towards Harkess Rocks, either fording Mill Burn or turning left to cross it at the road bridge and then turning right, back onto the beach. If the tide is out, walk along the rocks beneath the grass bank. If the sea is in an ugly mood, however, climb the bank and continue west along the roadside.

Harkess Rocks is carpeted by a layer of seaweed. In theory the different species should grow in definite zones, but most of the rocky coast of Northumberland shelves into the water too gradually to allow any definite bands to develop. Below the low water mark there are the oar-weeds, massive brown seaweeds with strong stems and 'holdfasts' attaching them to submerged rocks. They are rarely uncovered by the tide but after rough weather they may be ripped from their anchorage and thrown onto the shore. The intertidal seaweeds, adapted to the extremes of being baked half the time and submerged under cold salty water for the other half, are dominated by wracks. Channelled, spiral, bladder, serrated, and knotted wrack all survive in a confusing hotch-potch on these rocks.

Bladder Wrack

77

Stop at Stag Rock, close to the lighthouse.

The lighthouse is automatic and unmanned, like the one on Inner Farne. The promontory of Stag Rock projects north-east into the North Sea and seabirds often pass close by. Gannets are the most spectacular of these, having a 6 foot (2m) wingspan and a quixotic technique of plunge-diving for fish. The adults are brilliant-white with black wing tips whilst the juvenile birds are grey or speckled. Gannets nest on Bass Rock, some way to the north on the lip of the Firth of Forth, but disperse quite widely after the breeding season.

Bear left of the lighthouse. If the sea is very rough, follow the route outlined on page 24 until Budle Point is reached, but under normal circumstances it is perfectly safe to follow the shoreline. To do this, take the path at the base of the grassy bank, above the rocks. This takes you down to a small sandy bay. From there head westward, across a rocky shelf into another bay and towards Black Rock.

Most of the rocks are dolerite; the quarry face of Kittling Hill will probably be visible through a dip in the hills to the left. On the beach the dolerite is polished to a metallic blue-grey by the action of wind-blown sand.

If the visibility is good Holy Island will be a dominant feature on the skyline to the north west. The white cone-shaped structure on the extreme right (north-east) marks Emanuel Point, standing above a shallow cliff. Some way to the left can be seen the lime kilns and the castle, then the harbour, and finally the village with its priory and church. The two tall needles, sited on Guile Point rather than the island, are old navigation aids for the fishing fleet.

Continue round the headland to Budle Point.

Bamburgh, from Harkess Rocks

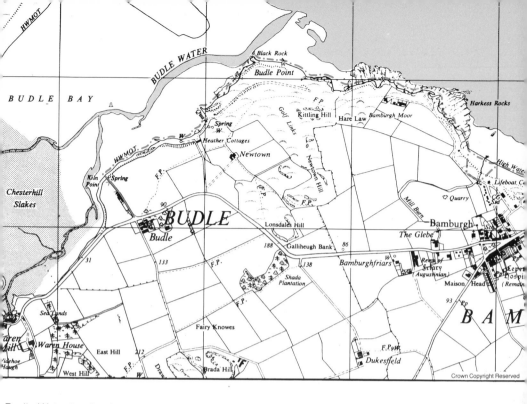

Budle Water has its channel on the south side of Budle Bay, just beyond Black Rock (another shelf of dolerite). The far bank – a sand ridge stretching over from Ross Back Sands – is a favourite roosting place for gulls and terns during the summer. Waders, ducks and geese use the site during the autumn and winter.

The coastline turns south-west, into Budle Bay. Continue along the upper shore towards the old quay.

The view of the hills to the west and north is particularly attractive, set behind the wide estuary sands. To the south-west stands Cheviot, 20 miles away; the Kyloe Hills, a dolerite and sandstone ridge covered with coniferous woodland, lie much closer to the north-west beyond Chesterhill Slakes. Finally, beyond Holy Island to the north lie Eyemouth and St. Abbs Head – one of the most dramatic cliffs in south-east Scotland.

Cross the dunes at the base of the quay, then rejoin the shoreline and continue south-west.

Whinstone (from Kittling Hill quarry) and grain were the important commodities shipped from this little harbour. Across Budle Bay is Ross Links, an immense area of stable sand dunes. It is part of the Lindisfarne National Nature Reserve and, because the sand is slightly more acidic than the dunes of Holy Island, provides a contrasting flora with several rarities.

The beach becomes rather shingly and before the bay broadens out to the left there is a National Nature Reserve sign and a track leading left.

The inner part of the bay, called Chesterhill Slakes, is rather muddy and is rich in shellfish – which is what many of the birds are searching for. According to William Whellan's Directory of 1855, the shores around Budle Bay 'abound with the largest and best cockles in the kingdom', but this is probably not the case today.

Turn left along the track, walk up past the farm cottage and out onto the B1342 at Budle.

Black Rock, looking over Budle Water to Ross Links and Holy Island ▷

Glossary

Barbican	Projecting watch-tower built to protect a castle gate.
Brigantine	Two masted vessel with square rigged foremast and fore-and-aft rigged main mast.
Burn	Small stream.
Byre	Cowshed.
Cairn	A pile of stones to mark a pre-historic burial site, or a route.
Carr	Marshy woodland.
Cist	Prehistoric stone coffin or burial chamber.
Coble	A small flat-floored fishing boat with a square stern.
Dolerite	Basic, coarsely-grained igneous rock.
Drove road	Old track, now generally grassed, once used when driving stock to market or new pastures.
Dyke	In the geological context, a ridge or band of volcanic rock formed when molten lava was forced through cracks and faults in the earth's crust.
Haugh	Flat land by riverside.
Heugh	A ridge, often ending abruptly.
Lonnen	Lane.
Motte & Bailey	Type of Norman castle, consisting of a steep-sided mount (motte), crowned with a wooden stockade (bailey) within which stood a wooden tower. Extra protection was provided in the form of ditches and pointed stakes interwoven with brambles.
Pele tower	Originally turf and wooden houses protected by palisades and moats; later pele towers were built of stone and were nearer to the castle in terms of importance.
Ridge & Furrow	Corrugated appearance of land thought to be caused by early forms of ploughing.
Sandstone	Sedimentary rock composed of compacted sand.
See	The office of Bishop of a particular diocese; a diocese.
Shale	Finely stratified rock resembling slate, but softer, consisting of consolidated mud or clay.
Steading	Farm house with farm buildings around it.
Studdle	A post or prop.
Synod	An ecclesiastical meeting or council.
Toxin	Poison.
Tumulus	A mound covering a burial.
Windblow	Erosion by wind.
Whinstone	Dolerite quarried from the Whin Sill for use as roadstone or building stone.
Wynd	Lane or narrow alley.

For further reading

BESIDE THE SEASIDE
by Tony Soper
B.B.C.

COLLINS POCKET GUIDE TO THE SEA SHORE
by J. Barrett & C.M. Yonge.
Collins

SEA SHORE NATURALISTS HANDBOOK
by Leslie Jackman
Hamlyn

HAMLYN GUIDE TO THE SEA SHORE
AND SHALLOW SEAS OF GREAT BRITAIN AND EUROPE
by A.C. Campbell
Hamlyn

THE SEA SHORE
by C.M. Yonge
Collins

A FIELD GUIDE TO THE INSECTS OF BRITAIN & NORTHERN EUROPE
by M. Chinery
Collins

THE BIRDS OF BRITAIN & EUROPE
by Heinzel, Fitter and Parslow
Collins

THE SEA BIRDS OF BRITAIN & IRELAND
by Cramp, Bourne and Saunders
Collins

ROCKS AND SCENERY FROM TYNE TO TWEED
by C.R. Warn
Frank Graham

CASTLES OF THE NORTHUMBERLAND COAST
by Frank Graham
Frank Graham

THE WILD FLOWER KEY
by F. Rose
Warne

OXFORD BOOK OF FLOWERLESS PLANTS
by F.H. Brightman
Oxford

Northumberland National Park and Countryside Publications

The publications listed here may be purchased from all good
booksellers in the north-east and from National Park or Country Park Information Centres.

IN THIS SERIES
WALKS IN THE CHEVIOT HILLS
WALKS IN THE HADRIAN'S WALL AREA
IN PREPARATION
WALKS IN COQUETDALE

PLESSEY – THE STORY OF A NORTHUMBRIAN WOODLAND
LOOK AROUND...HADRIAN'S WALL
A FIELD GUIDE TO THE HADRIAN'S WALL AREA
A FIELD GUIDE TO PLESSEY WOODS COUNTRY PARK
IN PREPARATION
LOOK AROUND...NORTHUMBERLAND COAST

If difficulty is experienced in obtaining copies please write to address below.
For general information about Northumberland National Park write, SAE please,to:
The National Park Officer, Eastburn, South Park, Hexham, Northumberland, NE46 1BS.
Comments and suggestions relating to this publication are welcomed.